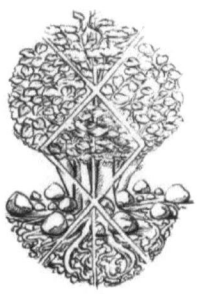

EUROPEAN ✻ NATIVE

LIVING-CIRCLE .mittelstand.de

The Frog King

& the children of Frya

A message from your ancestors.

Guido Eickhoff

LIVING-CIRCLE .mittelstand.de

LIVING-CIRCLE.mittelstand.de

Publisher: LIVING-CIRCLE.mittelstand.de
First edition: 05/2024 - Copyright Guido Eickhoff

Text: Guido Eickhoff Illustrations: Guido Eickhoff
Cover design: Guido Eickhoff
Back cover image: Thomas Arculeo
Editing: Ursula Frey, Heike Küsel
Publisher: "BoD · Books on Demand GmbH, In de Tarpen 42, 22848 Norderstedt"
Printed by: "Libri Plureos GmbH, Friedensallee 273, 22763 Hamburg".
© 2024 Guido Eickhoff
ISBN: 978-3-7597-5960-3

Bibliographic information of the German National Library: The German National Library lists this publication in the German National Bibliography; detailed bibliographic data is available on the Internet at dnb.dnb.de.

Contents

The Frog King 3

    Contents 5

    Thoughts 6

    Foreword 7

    Introduction 8

    The golden path. 11

    The frog, the well, the truth and the lie. 12

    The path of lies. 13

    The power of the word. 14

    The nature of truth. 15

& the children of Frya - *The children of free people* 17

    The king's daughter 18

    The frog 24

    The forest 28

    The lime tree 30

    The fountain 32

    The golden ball 48

The Frog King & the children of Frya 61

    1 - The indigenous consciousness - Cosmology 63

    2 - The free people 71

    3 - The descent of mankind 77

    4 - The guardians of wisdom 83

    5 - The secret of being human - The companion (Gesell) 89

    6 - The secret of humanity - the indigenous European circular culture 97

    7 - Human consciousness - the hero's journey 103

    8 - The turn of man - The promise 109

    9 - The turning point of humanity - Responsibility 117

    10 - The turning of the worlds - The Ragnarök 123

    11 - The solution 131

    12 - The initiates 137

    13 - The rebirth 145

    The conclusion is the key. 149

    Sources, book list 150

    Our initiatives 152

    A project by LIVING-CIRCLE.mittelstand.de 153

    Books - LIVING-CIRCLE.mittelstand.de: 154

Thoughts

For

Katharina,

Tim, Emily, Johanna, Karl, Kiara, Aurin, Alana Fee, Ylvi Marie
and all the other rainbow children,
especially the coming generations of this world.

Many thanks to

Ursula Frey and Heike Küsel for their wonderful support and clarity,

Thomas Arculeo for his true patience and wisdom

and all those who have walked this path before me and left their mark.

Without them, this book would never have been possible.

Foreword

"You are indigenous. There is no other way but to be indigenous. Look in the mirror and look at your eyes, you will find all the generations of your ancestors there, in your genes."

"Humanity has reached a point where our survival as a species must be decided, how we are to survive as a whole. It is not a question of whether we are indigenous or not, it is about the quality of life according to the laws of nature and about diversity in unity guiding future generations and contributing to the survival of humanity as a species.

To be indigenous is to continue the purpose of your genetic heritage as a species, each individual, with the goal of the well being of the species of humanity. Yes, humans have made mistakes, that is part of learning and evolution.

Being indigenous is not a question, it is everyone's responsibility to recognize this responsibility, just as every flower, tree, stone and drop of water plays its part in supporting life in unity in diversity.

The future of humanity is in danger. The Earth herself is calling her children to return to the "indigenous way" to recognize their role as part of natural law, to support life and unite as one species."

Thomas Arculeo, White Eagle
Elders of the Haudenosaunee (Iroquois), Six Nations

Introduction

Thank you for your attention.

It is still believed today that fairy tales were written for children, that they are meant to stimulate the imagination or leave moral instructions. The opposite is the case.

Fairy tales are a fine art of coding. If you tell your children or friends "The Tale of the Frog Prince", you will not only be able to pass on the true meaning after reading this book. When we delve into the old "hidden" knowledge of our ancestors, it will also open up and explain new meanings about your own personal life and our society. It is the chance to experience a new way of thinking about a reality that you never thought possible before. In its simplicity, if understood correctly, it offers solutions to many of life's stressful questions, which have also opened up a completely more peaceful, freer, more determined attitude to life for me. It contains a cornucopia of information that will have an epigenetic influence on our society and opens the way to a unique cultural evolution when the knowledge finally spreads.

Fairy tales, legends and myths teach entire contexts of natural science, history, politics, ethnology, psychology, cosmology, quantum physics, economics, social culture, education, development of consciousness, and and and ... which would take years to learn using "school methods". Because every single word, every image, every metaphor, every letter of a story, a fairy tale, in turn contains a very deep universe of wisdom and truth. You just need the right perspective to recognize them. Because they contain so much profound wisdom, it was sometimes difficult for me to decide which information to pass on.

That's why I chose the Frog King. Because this fairy tale offers crucial information for peaceful and valuable solutions that are of decisive importance for our present and future. In this fairy tale, I have also only referred to the most essential symbols and interpretations, as the depth of knowledge would go beyond the scope of a book.

The knowledge of the meaning of the true history of indigenous Europe, your genetic heritage, the land of our ancestors (people of all peoples of the world), has been hidden, concealed and covered up. But it becomes obvious when you are among the initiated. Once you have the key, a new world opens up.

"It's in your genes. You are Indigenous."

It's like a call that you've known since childhood, which becomes quieter from time to time or fades away because your attention changes. But it's always there and it's getting louder and louder at this time.

That was the beginning of my journey in search of the source that led to this book and on which I now want to take you.

Guido Eickhoff

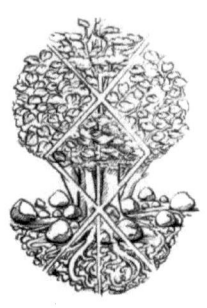

EUROPEAN�֍NATIVE

The golden path.

"When people recognize the primordial, for many forgotten, ancient wisdom that has been lost over the centuries, they perceive the world of nature anew, in all its wonderful beauty and its magnificent diversity.

Enlightened, inspired people have a different life, their inner world changes. The soul, spirit and conscience blossom harmoniously in it, allowing the flower of the fern to bloom in the heart of each individual."
SCOURCE: Santia Weden

The path to truth is often not easy. In the ancient wisdom, the world, nature, we find the legacy of the indigenous Europeans, your ancestors. This book is about the cultural evolution of the next generations and the influence and pearls of an ancient culture that will have a serious impact on today's and tomorrow's economy, politics, education, communication and culture.

This book will take you back to your roots.
Indigenous Europe, the land of your genetic ancestors, the knowledge in your genes.

"You are indigenous. There is no other way but to be indigenous. Look in the mirror and look at your eyes, you will find all the generations of your ancestors there, in your genes."
Thomas Arculeo

The frog, the well, the truth and the lie.

"The truth and the lie meet on the road. The lie says: "Today is a wonderful day!" The truth looks up to the sky and sighs, because the day was really beautiful.

They come to a well. The lie says: "The water is very nice, let's take a bath together!" Truth tests the water and agrees.

They undress and start bathing. Suddenly, the lie gets out of the water, puts on the truth's clothes and runs away. The truth climbs out of the well and looks for the lie to get her clothes back.

The world, seeing the truth naked, averts its eyes with contempt and anger. The poor truth returns to the well in shame and disappears forever.

Since then, the lie has been traveling around the world - disguised as truth - and satisfying the needs of society. For the world has no desire whatsoever to encounter the naked truth. "
Unknown

The truth about the history of Europe and the true nature of this world has been hidden. As Democritus said: *"We know nothing of the truth, for the truth is deep in the well."*

However, so that every generation can find the truth, it has been shown "naked" in myths, fairy tales and songs, but not visible to most people. However, those who are initiated into the knowledge of our primal culture, natural science, metaphors, the code of language, runes or the primal/root language can decipher it. But it often seems so unbelievable that we prefer to believe the lies.

The path of lies.

"At one time - it is said - every child had to learn the "Good Language" - the theodic, divine language - because it ensured that if you did not speak the truth, you blushed with shame and began to stutter.

But since deceitful priests and wicked princes wanted to live their own inclinations without regard to the laws of justice, they began to invent other languages so that they could speak about their wicked and unworthy affairs in the presence of anyone else without betraying themselves by stammering and without showing a blush on their faces.

Thus men lost the ability to 'be free' and 'speak truth' through their words, and so virtue has departed from their midst, wisdom has followed and freedom has vanished, concord has been lost and discord has taken its place; love has fled and shamelessness sits at the table with envy, and where justice once reigned, the sword now reigns."
From Oera Linda

The history of mankind, as it is taught in schools and science today, is very different from that which your ancestors and all the indigenous peoples of this world tell and still know. In Europe in particular, this indigenous knowledge and the wisdom associated with it was almost completely wiped out. Time and again, people who wanted to revive this knowledge were persecuted, killed, ridiculed, imprisoned and mocked.

This book is not about judgment, prejudice or condemnation. It is about portraying a world that reconnects and reconnects us with our own peaceful indigenous culture and that of all indigenous peoples. With the aim of making the best of the past, for the present, the future and the next generations.

"The truth is naked, like the frog that is deep in the well and can now come out to show itself."

The power of the word.

Natural language developed from a system of sounds and tones that first referred to parts of the body and then to objects in the environment. It is a metaphor language, as we still find it in Old High German. This means that there are several possible interpretations of a single word and an even greater number due to the letters. (Example: crown = crown of the head, but also crown of a tree, crown of a king, crown of a bottle, crown as a means of payment) Thus certain word images, such as chariot, plate or fountain, are connected with scientific laws, numerical values, ideological, psychological, spiritual, historical, cosmological and many other contexts of meaning, which become apparent from the so-called "hidden/occult secret teachings". But everything is based on the indigenous European natural sciences of prehistoric times. It is like a code that needs to be deciphered. The title of the fairy tale alone provides clues as to what lies behind the story. If you look at it from the perspective of letters or ancient runes, which served as symbols for sounds, i.e. frequencies.

(FROG) FROSCH - ᚠ ᚱ ᛟ ᛋ ᚲ ᚺ

ᚠ	"Children of the times of freedom and abundance,
ᚱ	Set out on the path of justice
ᛟ	your heritage and your home.
ᛋ	You will find success and new vitality,
ᚲ	through the renewal of knowledge,
ᚺ	to nature and your healing."

(KING) KÖNIG - ᚲ ᛟ ᛖ ᚾ ᛁ ᚷ

ᚲ	"The renewal of knowledge,
ᛟ	about your heritage, your home,
ᛖ	trust and humanity
ᚾ	who are in need and distress,
ᛁ	will be frozen for so long,
ᚷ	until giving comes first again."

"The Frog King's message is dedicated to you, the child of Frya, to you, the descendant of the free people of Europe, to the knowledge and heritage in your genes." Guido Eickhoff

The nature of truth.

The lie travels around with the clothes of truth.

The clothes of truth are freedom, peace, knowledge and prosperity for all people. They have been promised to people for many millennia.

But when we look behind the façade, we realize something else. The world and the history of mankind that we know consists of many external, small and large wars and sacrifices. From division and fragmentation in many ages and right up to the present day. This then leads to inner wars and sacrifices of every single human being over many generations and right up to you.

You will find the lie where ideologies and laws are devised by people, stories are written by victors and in promises that are not kept. It is the ideas of individuals that are supposed to pacify the needs of many through hierarchies. They are reflections and distortions of the values that once applied to everyone. But even the spoken word has been distorted.

You find the truth in nature and its laws of life. The truth of nature demands responsibility for freedom, peace, knowledge and prosperity from everyone, it is the conscience. You will find the naked truth where you least expect it. Right under your nose. Look in the mirror.

Because you are not aware of your own greatness.

The history of mankind in Europe and the wisdom of nature can be found in the culture of the circle, your genes and the stories of your ancestors.

The most important identifiers:

The truth is that behind the old fairy tales, myths and legends lie secret messages, messages from your ancestors, scientific connections and indigenous wisdom that should remain secret until the time is right. It seems that the time has come for you.

It is called balding. From bald, as bald head or shaved head or to make an area treeless. In other words, something that has been removed, shortened, shaved or even coiffed. There are whole worlds of knowledge behind them.

King:	Cosmos | (king = rig = light of life, guiding ray)
Daughters:	Female
Royal child:	Earth Humanity (Youngest Daughter)
Frog:	Free man
Sun:	Time, energy
Golden:	Light, energy
Ball:	Life - Conscience - Cycles - Energy wheel
Fountain:	Stone circle - Knowledge - Time quantity
	Knowledge (Giant) - Consciousness (Dragon) - Fate (Norne)
Castle:	Ancestral seat, star fortress
Forest:	Habitat, tribal theory
Lime tree:	Tree of life, family tree
Water:	Genetic knowledge
Gesell:	5/0, Community/Wralda
Bed:	1, Father, fire
Mug:	2, Mother, Earth
Table:	3, Creation, water
Plates:	4, Child, air
Marble staircase:	Mission of life
Blackboard:	Circle of ancestors
Wall:	Turn of the world (Ragnarök)
Heinrich:	Twin self, the cosmic human (Heimdall, Rig)
Horse, steed:	Mind power, consciousness
Eight:	8, Infinity, respect, mindfulness, authenticity
Trolley:	Body, scale, cradle
Empire:	Abundance, freedom
Lord:	Happy, Life
Rig:	Life energy

The children of Frya

The children of free people

The interpretation of words and truth.

The king's daughter

Earth Humanity - Youngest Daughter (Jung = Jul)

Many thousands of years ago, before the concepts of Germanic tribes and Celts existed, your ancestors lived as free and peaceful people on this planet we now call Earth. Their land stretched from the North Sea in the north to Russia in the south. From sunrise to the east, the Baltic Sea and to the Mediterranean Sea to sunset in the west.

At that time, the world still turned differently. Because - over 4000 years ago - the world made a small leap and the poles realigned themselves once again. Why is the North Sea still called the North Sea if it is in the west? These are cycles in which the world and the centuries move. They still knew that the earth itself is a living being that has good and bad days. The place where they were to be found is now called Europe, or perhaps „EUeR OPA" (Your Grandfather) would be a better name.

They lived peacefully in many small communities, villages, castles and star fortresses. They had folk, castle and village mothers and fathers. Well-educated, wise and good-natured women and men who gave advice. Life, knowledge and law were based on the Jul.

The Jul [Jung, Jul - The winter solstice. Refers to the North Star and the North Pole, as the genetic origin of mankind and the source of the wisdom of natural science] is the wheel, the circle of the year, but also the Christmas star, which we can still recognize today in ancient ruins and stone circles. A fire, a lamp, always burned in the center of the circle. It was often found in a tower in the middle of the village or castle circle. This was the symbol and center of all their wisdom. The few laws they needed were also carved on the towers, as they were a people of high conscience. The writing originated from the wheel because they later feared that the knowledge, which was otherwise only passed on orally, would be forgotten.

They inherited the knowledge of the circle from their ancestors. The circle and the flame in the center is the most powerful sign of the energy of this earth, the cosmos and also in you.

It is their legacy, an ancient social society and a prosperous economic and educational culture that lived more than just in harmony with nature. The most advanced teachings and thus the roots of our civilization lie in these indigenous natural sciences. They were the basis for epoch-making leaps in the development of our civilization. The deep connection with nature and the wisdom of the laws of nature were among the most progressive and prosperous role models in the history of Europe and should now be reintroduced.

Everything in this culture revolves around the cycle and the energy of light. Yule is an expression and description of the male fire, the power and free energy that also gives life to your body. You can also feel this energy inside you, like a golden ball. Like a "magic" lamp in the Christmas star of the fortresses, like the fire in the circle of friends. Like the sun in our planetary system, like the center of all universes in the cosmos. It is in every human being, every animal, every plant, in our earth. It is always "shining" and carries all wisdom within it. We also call it Rig, from the Irish origin of the word king and the Heimdall of Norse mythology or the faithful Henry of this fairy tale. It is the king, the true ruler of a wonderful realm that illuminates every life like a guiding ray. It is connected to everything that is and everything that will be. Eternal.

So they lived peacefully and in harmony with everything in nature. Because they knew that everything is connected to everything else and never ends. Water, earth, air and fire were their friends. From which everything, including themselves, was created. Everything was connected to the ancient and that is why they called it **Wralda**. Which means: (**Wr** = U+U+r) the primeval everything that is there, they also called it "spirit [spirit (germ. „Geist") = G - gift, E - human, I - creation, S - sun, T - friend, tribe]". Wralda is contained in the entire cosmos down to the smallest microbe. Today it is called quanta, which are neutral in themselves. Vralda is in everything and everything is in Vralda. This is one of its deepest wisdoms, which still holds true today. Over time, it has been given many names: Ether, Akasha, Orenda, Orgone, Chi, Plasma, Quantum Field and many more. Your ancestors knew it was always good and neutral, an invisible treasure. But to this day, some people turn good, god, got, into god. In the course of time, good and god became a symbol for super-beings. What used to be simple natural science became a symbol of domination, subjugation and irritation through magicians and priests. Everyone did their work and deeds for the good of the community. Their daily work was varied, there were times of the day of fire, of the spirit where they learned. Times of the earth, the body, where they practiced their craft and martial arts. Times of water, the soul, where they philosophized. Times of the air, der community, where they danced, played and pursued the arts.

They knew the truths of cycles, tides and stories. This knowledge was passed on by the wise women and men of old to their children, as it was to their ancestors, through the stone circle. They passed on their knowledge of the cycle of nature in this world, the spiral of life and the wisdom of emergence. Emergence means: "Every single thing together makes more than the whole and everything grows from within". So they learned everything there was to learn from nature and it was passed down orally from their ancestors. They used nature to explain everything and told it in stories to make it easier to remember. Their knowledge of nature, life and the cosmos was immense, much more than we can even imagine today.

They learned 4000 years ago, not only to read, write and calculate. They also learned crafts, martial arts, psychology, biology, cosmology, technology, nautics and much more. Children were their greatest asset and it was even one of their first sacred laws that everything they did was only for the benefit of their children.

The free, conscientious people knew no gods, no God, demons, spirits, magic, sorcery, sacrificial rituals or miracles. They were trained in the indigenous natural sciences, which were much more highly developed than today's science. Their simple understanding of astrophysics, quantum mechanics, electromagnetism, naturopathy and many other natural sciences is being confirmed and increasingly "rediscovered" by today's science.

PHOTON

ERDE

KOSMOS

"Wralda, who alone is good and eternal, made the beginning, then came time; time created all things, including the earth (Irtha). Irtha gave birth to all grasses, herbs, trees, all the good and all the bad creatures."

"Wralda is the most ancient and super-ancient, for It created all things. Vralda is all in all, for It is eternal and infinite. Vralda is everywhere present, but nowhere to be seen: therefore this Being is called Spirit.

All we can see of Him are the creatures that come and go through His life: for from Vralda all things come and all things return. From Vralda comes the beginning and the end, all things merge into Him. Wralda is the one all-powerful being [Wesen (Middle High German wësen: stay, way of life, quality, situation)], for all other power is borrowed from him and returns to him. All powers come from Wralda, and all powers return to Him.

Therefore, He alone is the creating Being, and there is nothing created except Her. Vralda put eternal statutes, that is, laws, into all created things, and there are no good laws unless they are formed according to them. But although everything is in Vralda, the wickedness of man is not in Him. Wickedness comes from laziness, carelessness and stupidity. Vralda is wisdom, and the laws she has created are the books from which we can learn, and there is no wisdom to be found nor gathered except this.

People can see many things, but Wralda sees all things. Men can open up many things, but everything is open to Vralda. Men are male and female, but Vralda created both. Humans mine [Minne (Old High German minna: helping, caring, friendly) Isn't it strange that the saying "to make someone minna" means the opposite (to blame someone in a humiliating way, to put someone down roughly)] and hate, but Wralda alone is just. Therefore, Vralda alone is good, and there is nothing good except Him. With the Jul (wheel) all created things change and change, but the good alone is unchanging. Because Vralda is good, it cannot change, and because it remains, it alone is essence and everything else is appearance."

From Oera Linda

This text is over 4000 years old and already explains the quantum theory (quantization of electromagnetic radiation) which was only "invented" by Max Plank on 14 December 1900?

Traditional indigenous European natural science:

Nature as a model, key and path of knowledge of laws, has provided the true basis for the flourishing cultural development of mankind for several thousand years.

The frog

Free man

They were a happy people, the frosk people, frosk like the frog[1].
They were experienced sailors, traders, forest people who lived in a communal and circular culture.
They felt like kings, but did not behave like them.
They traveled as seafarers across the seas along all the coasts of the world.
They spread peace, knowledge, wisdom and connected with all people.

---

[1] Frog,Froh, frosk, frosch, have the self-similar sound and sound stem. This is a secret for decoding in the "original language". The letters or runes that were to be "murmured" (F, R, O, H) in turn have a meaning. F is the seed - R is the energy, law - O is the spirit, thought, universe - H is the cosmos, treasure. This is how the sounds describe the scientific process of "happiness". But also the evolution of all life, for which the frog stands as a symbol of evolution from water to land animal.

The people of the Happy People were all of high nobility, which in truth means of high truthfulness, nobility and wisdom. They were noble people who knew the value of their own lives and whose goal was the knowledge of absolute truth. They did not allow themselves to be shackled by the outward appearance of the material world and therefore knew very well what freedom was. Those who did not abide by it were excluded from the community. They were noble people who always spoke the truth, as their cultivated language meant that lies were immediately recognizable on their faces. Later, they were mocked for their "blue-eyedness". Their nature and their few rules always applied to the knowledge of the cosmos, nature and the truth. They were all equal. The wisest and humblest were their advisors, the oldest and most experienced decided in joint council. No one called themselves king, queen or leader. In legends we hear of them - the radiant ones - but more on this later, in the form of the faithful Henry.

These happy noble people were your great-great-great-great-grandparents, that is, about 200 times 200 parents of your parents before your time. Everyone has two parents, four grandparents, eight great-grandparents and so on - the number of ancestors doubles with each generation. After just a few generations, the family trees of people living in completely different parts of the world overlap. So the whole world is your kin and part of your ancestry.

This is also your tribe and among them there were many tribes. They are the family tree of your genes, so we come to the word generations. The genes are what is generated or created from 5 elements, fire, water, earth, air and vralda, from which everything that exists in nature is created. When a person leaves, they become the 5 elements again and nourish their offspring. So everything is contained in everything and connected with each other and deserves your respect. The grandmother as well as the daisy. Because we are all part of the whole and so the whole becomes more than its individual parts.

They called themselves the children of Frya.

You too are, in one way or another, a child of Frya. Today they are still known as Frisians, which is close to the word peace and describes them very well. Because that was her constant endeavor. Her name also tells of her origin, the Fry-a = Frey-en, the free people. Who tolerated no one above or below them.

Frya is regarded as their "original mother". There are many stories and legends about her and her brother Fryr. We find stories of Fryr and Frya as the first humans on earth. Sometimes they are also described as "twin souls". Or rather, the male, positive, giving principle and the female, negative, attracting principle of electromagnetism and quantum mechanics. Even today, people try to turn them into gods, but if you understand the meaning, their names and descriptions take on a much deeper meaning. This is also the principle of fairy tales. To use sound-like letters for respective principles or events. Fry = Free. The ending -a, is the feminine, absorbing, life-giving principle of the (A-tem) breath and -r, is the driving, dominating, masculine principle of solar energy.

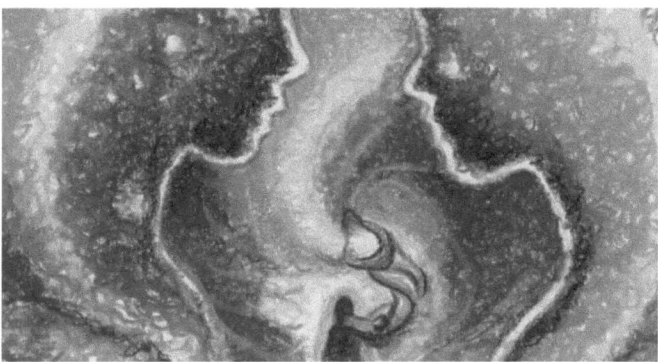

So we find about Fryr, his name is also Froh, which is synonymous with Lord. He stands for the young sun god who is born at the low point of the sun, Jul, our Christmas season. He is the free man and the suitor who, as the Eddic Skirnismal[Skirnismal - Skirnir (actual spelling Skírnir) metaphors of Norse mythology for worldly wisdom .] wooing Gerda, the earth. He is also described in fairy tales as a representative of the golden age in the form of the "Frog King".

His sister Frya, (Old Norse "mistress") or Frigg, can be found as the goddess of fertility, spring, happiness and love in the Norse myths of the Edda.

Above all, however, Frya stands for the founder and mother of the children of Frya, the free peoples of Europe. She is also the **"King's Daughter"** and thus the preceding humanity of Europe[2]. This is what we find in the Oera Linda, an episodic chronicle of the wars and migrations of the European people who populated the whole of Europe long before the migration of peoples. It describes very precisely the events from 2,194 BC to 803 AD, the truth and confirmation of which we also find in the songs and stories of all the indigenous peoples of the world.

Frya and Fryr also stand for the principles of two social orders. The female, passive, preserving, egalitarian, matriarchal[3] order and the male, active, conquering, hierarchical, patriarchal order. While passive societies stood for advanced civilizations and peace in our prehistoric times, active societies have caused the opposite and confusion right up to the present day.

But because our ancestors knew no gods, Frya's children stand for the truly free and peaceful people, the indigenous, the one-born or better nature-born, who knew the mysteries of light, energy and the cosmos. Whose wisdom we still know in the indigenous teachings in all four directions, only here in Europe, in the north, no longer.

---

[2] The Danube civilization as a scientifically proven "matriachal" culture (Harald Haarmann) in the period from approx. 5,000 BC to approx. 3,500 BC is also a contemporary witness here.

[3] „Women think in terms of connection and networking. Men think in hierarchies, rope teams and alliances" Source: Vera F. Birkenbihl Our brain: The right, female brain hemisphere, organizes overall contexts, creativity and emotionality, the male, left brain hemisphere, details, drawers and logic. A lack of coherence or balance between the brain hemispheres leads to disharmony. Our autonomic nervous system: The "male" sympathetic nervous system regulates bodily functions in stressful situations and is responsible for arousal and activity. The "female" parasympathetic system regulates bodily functions in phases of rest and recovery and is responsible for regeneration.

The energy pathway system from yoga: Pingala, male, sympathetic and Ida, female, parasympathetic, Sushuma is the central nervous system. Neutrality and balance in the nervous system sustains life.

The forest

Habitat, tribal theory

Many of your ancestors, the happy people, the free people, lived in the forests. The forest was sacred to them, because they found themselves in it.

Everything is nature, and so are the trees, plants, mushrooms and animals in your nature. Today, the forest scares many people, but at a time when the forest was large and powerful, people also understood life through the forest. Even today, stories about the tree of life and the tree of wisdom can be found all over the world. These stories have their origin in the forest, because it was in the forest that they found the whole understanding of the world and of life. The tree is the family tree, the village, the community. In its trunk, from the roots, the water is drawn from the earth into the leaves. The sun converts the water in the leaves into sugar and thus supplies the roots. Everything is a cycle.

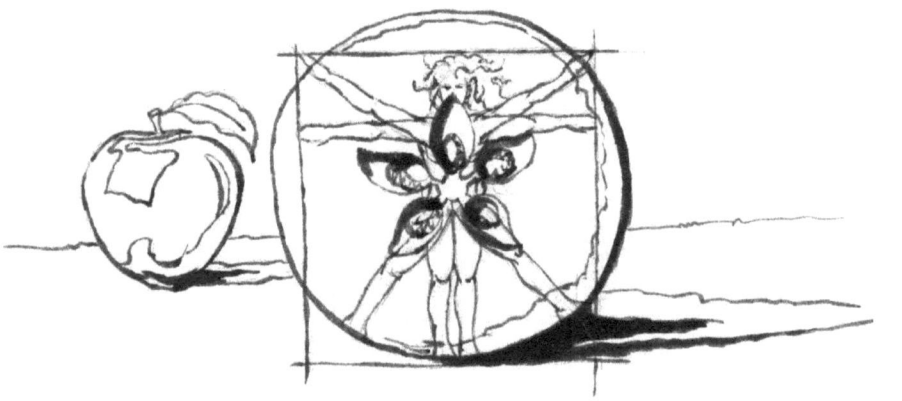

The leaves represent the children of the future, the young shoots that feed their roots. The roots are the people, the stories of the ancestors, the cornerstones. Those who forget their roots have no future. The mycelium, the mushrooms are the communication and logistics, the nerve network of the forest or the internet of the world. We find many such teachings in all indigenous cultures.

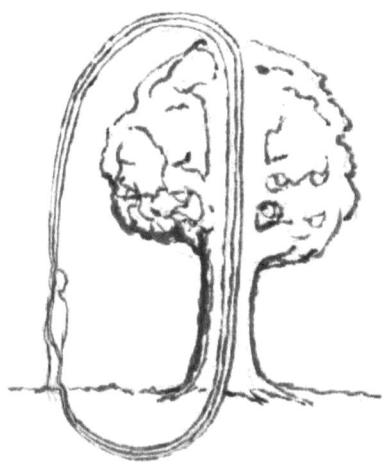

The people of the forest were of exceptional stature, strength and intelligence. Some stood over 2.20 meters tall. Their food was the forest, the herbs their pharmacy. The combination of body, mind, soul and community and the close connection to the wisdom of nature made the Free People into very special people of courage, strength and wisdom. For they knew that there is no death. Everything is a cycle and everything is connected.

"Death does not exist and with this knowledge its fear also disappears. No human being has ever died. They became light and as such they still exist. The secret is that these particles of light return to their original state. To one of the former energies."
Nikola Tesla

They knew about the power of water, the primordial and healing springs. As a storehouse of knowledge, teacher, elixir of life and fountain of youth. Because water is the driving force of nature. That is why they were not only excellent sailors, but also powerful, vital people full of life energy and high physical intelligence.

Their children learned martial arts early on as a defense and life strategy. For self-control and to increase the vitality of body and mind, because they were not conquerors. They were peaceful warriors. Trained in this way, they became feared opponents. Their high level of physical intelligence and their knowledge of the power of invisible space not only made them appear superhuman, but also manifested itself in their intelligent strategies. They have survived many centuries and defended their land.

The lime tree

Tree of life, family tree

"Where the lime tree grows, heaven and earth meet. Its remedies are gentle and carry the power of the "lime worm" of the earth dragon (consciousness), the earth mother. For our ancestors, it was the tree of Frya, the gentle "goddess" of love, marriage and the peaceful coexistence of the clan. The lime tree was seen as the protective, nurturing, tenderly guarding heart of the goddess, the nurse, the queen. As Frya's tree, it was said to gently but clearly bring the truth to light, and until the end of the 18th century, court and thing meetings were held under the lime trees.

Lime trees can live for up to 1500 years (they outlast the ages). In contrast to oak, they hardly store any tannins and rot from the inside out - they become hollow. In old age, however, the lime tree often suddenly develops a completely new vitality, rising again like a phoenix from the ashes. It drives young tree roots from the branches through the old, hollow trunk towards the ground and anchors them in the soil. The fresh roots provide a new, magnificent crown. In this way, it rejuvenates itself from the inside out as it ages. "

From: Trees and the healing power of the forest (Bäume und die Heilende Kraft des Waldes), Adelheid Lingg

So the lime tree in the fairy tale shows us that the connection between generations has a very high power that has been taken from us over the centuries.

There are many types of trees and teachings, e.g. the oak for strength, the birch that brings everything into flow. The spruce teaches us that we don't have to look for love on the outside. It shows us the source of light within ourselves. - "If you have questions, sit by a spruce tree" and many more teachings. They showed the children life.

The old people used the trees of life to explain the wisdom of life and knew the power inherent in the lime tree - it alleviates everything. For this reason, there was a lime tree in the middle of every village square. The Common Eight (from "common", not common, another twist, eight - "those for whom one has respect"), the council meeting or Thing, was elected by the people. They gathered under the tree to deliberate.

They were a happy, cheerful people who often and gladly celebrated the successes of their energy. These celebrations took place under the lime tree. They danced in a circle around the tree, because the circle gave them a safe space, it was their spatial power. It was like an intoxication that they could create from within, without intoxicants.

Because there was no time for them, their ancestors and their future descendants, including you, were always there in their thoughts. Because nothing is faster than a thought. Everything they did, they did with them. So they deliberated on every deed and every decision, not just for themselves, but for everyone there!

The tree also stands for the World Tree [World Tree: Yggdrasil as the "Tree of Life", is a metaphor and a teaching path for the "spiritual-scientific" (non-visible) self-similar principle of energy effect. We find it in the cosmic laws, in the natural laws and also in the laws of man. It represents the idea of life, death and rebirth. Its roots reach deep into the underworld and its foliage extends into the heavenly spheres. It embodies the cycle of life and reminds us that everything is interwoven. The tree can teach us to live in harmony with nature and other living beings.

The tree as a symbol of peace can still be found today in the culture of the American "Iroquois" Haudenousaunee (people of the longhouse) and is mentioned in the songs of Deganawida[]. He was a peacekeeper, a peacemaker. A shining white man who rode on a boat made of "stone". He was a child of Frya, counselor and prophet who prophesied the unification of all Iroquois because they had common ancestors and similar languages. This was then fulfilled by Hiawatha, the Great Peacekeeper, through the unification of the hostile tribes and the founding of the Iroquois Confederacy. Which in turn served as a model for today's democratic parliaments, "discovered" by Benjamin Franklin. Unfortunately, it was only partially transferred, as the most important matriarchal original principles were not adopted. This is why we now live in a pyramidal culture of domination instead of an egalitarian circular culture. For people today, these seem to be dreamy images and nonsensical thoughts that keep them in captivity, the knowledge too simple-minded, unreal and no longer appropriate for today's world. But I have to consider this. There must be a good reason why people are so desperate to hide, suppress or denigrate the truth about our culture. This is just a grain of sand in a universe that hides far greater things and you will find out.

The fountain

Stone circle - Knowledge - Time quantity
Knowledge (Giant) - Consciousness (Dragon) - Fate (Norne)

The fountain is a source and a symbol of the origin.

A well is a stone circle - The stone circle is still today, more than a symbol for the knowledge and teaching culture of all free indigenous advanced civilizations and prehistoric times in the north of this earth, from Western and Eastern Europe to Siberia. The official megalithic objects such as Stonehenge and their interpretations do not come close to reflecting reality. All over the world you can find these legacies and their principles, the highly intellectual cosmic teachings and practical application of our ancestors.

The water in the well, which makes up 70% of the earth and mankind, is the symbol of knowledge. It is in the genes, the cells, the whole body, every plant, every tree in the entire earth. Your body has around 70 trillion cells. The DNA in every cell in your body can store around 1 million terabytes of data per square millimeter, as science has just discovered. It is a "light information store", a huge "quantum computer" that can easily store the information of many generations. (Picture[4])

---

[4] Leppen spring, Austria. "The closer you get to the spring, the purer and clearer the water becomes."

In the mythology of the Norse cultures, the Edda [The Edda - source for Norse mythology from the 13th century], we find detailed references to the deeper meaning through three wells.

Fountain 1 - Mimir's (Giant) Well - Knowledge and Wisdom

This is the source of wisdom. Access to deeper insight: the memory of what has happened since the beginning of creation and the vision of what still has to happen. Everything is preserved in the well of the giant Mimir, including the collective unconscious. (Picture[5])

5 Um 1100, Kyffhäuser fountain Germany, the deepest handmade castle fountain in the world (176 m). The Barbarossa saga

Fountain 2 - Nidhöggr (Dragon) Well- Knowledge and Consciousness

Becoming aware of the old battles with the "dragons[6]" - the inner battle with our conscience (fears) and the outer battles of wars, catastrophes and conquests. This is also meant in the historical references (mythology) about the real battle of Siegfried (Europe) and the dragon (Asia). The Hun invasion, the Magyar (Hungarian) invasion, the Roman invasion and many more. The well points to the realization of the true legacies of our ancestors and the uncovering of our true past. Here we find the reasons for all the traumas of all generations, but also the solutions that our ancestors left behind. (Picture[7])

---

[6] The amygdala is the seat of our fear and desire center, it "fires" our emotions, overrides the mind and conscious action. In dreams, we process our fears and desires, i.e. our passions.

[7] Around 1600, lindworm well (lindworm well), Klagenfurt, Germany. The Siegfried saga

Fountain3 - Urd (Norns) Well - Fate

The (Schick-sal) Destiny (in the ahd., fate, holy order). We find in the word fate the original meaning as destiny. Very positive in its intention, not tainted with false ideas and illusions. It is the human ability to create a universal, sacred, healing, harmonious order.

The guardians of the Urd source are the three Norns. They are called Urd (fate, past), Verdandi (the becoming, present) and Skuld (guilt, future). For this alone, there are many meaningful connections to the doctrine of origins, also in connection with other mythologies. Those who recognize the knowledge of their own origin and the principles of nature gain control over their own self-determined life. Cause, effect, guilt. (More on the distortion of guilt later). (Picture[8])

---

[8] Around 1900, Fountain of the Norns, Munich (Nornenbrunnen, München). Die Yggdrasilsaga

The indigenous principles and knowledge of your ancestors never came from "magic", "sorcery", "rituals", "spirits", "gods" to whom you can pass the buck. They found the origin in natural science. They recognized that everything in this cosmos exists in a perfect harmony of self-similar principles and can be achieved through skillful action with a higher perception and attention. According to the simple principles of cause and effect.

The well is also the superconscious, subconscious and unconscious. The dark water in the well is the way down into the darkness, the hypnotic[9] A state in which we can learn more about ourselves. But also the hypnotic state (hypno = sleep) into which many people can be put. It is the state of sacred play. When we observe the children more again, we recognize their sacred play. There they connect with what they have experienced in this world and with what they still have left from their origins. It is the conscience of our ancestors that they still carry within them.

In this way, the fairy tale shows that we adults in particular can go deeper within ourselves. We should question our conscience and define whether the world we live in is really the best we can achieve. Or whether we are not making too many compromises. If we only go back deeper in time in our history, we will not only find many clues for us, but completely different ways of thinking and the true spirit of our ancestors. You will recognize the truth, because it is stored within you. Nevertheless, it also requires the "deed" to achieve the effect. The triskel or the trivium[10] are the signposts here.

The water of the fountain is the mirror to yourself and the memory, the memory of your ancestors in your genes. But only when you look deeper can you discover them. It is the source, the origin that needs to be fathomed, but many people do not go far enough. What real freedom means lies hidden deep in the dark, in you and in the history of mankind.

_____

[9] Hypno = sleep (darkness) - Some people consider hypnosis to be "magic". But it is the scientific understanding of the frequencies of the brain and their influence on the "mind". This can be used to heal and manipulate consciousness.

[10] Trivium - The trivium (Latin for "three ways") refers to the remnants of the indigenous scientific teaching methodology (grammar - perceive, dialectic - understand, rhetoric - pass on).

In the depths of a well, we are also shown the illusion of time.

In the fairy tale of „Frau Holle" (Mrs. Holle), too, we still find the true indication of the true "understanding of time and spirit" and the symbol of the well. Gold and Pitch Mary descend through the well into the heaven of Frau Holle, the dream world, the superconscious, and through a gate back up to earth, the unconscious. This twisting, hidden, reflects the scientific understanding of reality of the indigenous peoples. The image seems somewhat confusing, but the 8 of the Möbius strip is a good symbol for this.

The fountain is like a portal through time when you are in your daydreams or dreaming at night. Time outside moves differently than in your dreams. It changes your sense of time. You can descend deeper and deeper and still end up in Mrs. Holle's heavenly garden. When I bear witness to your ancestors, as I have just done, were they not with you at the same moment? Did you live with them? When I testify of the next seven generations, can you imagine how you will live with them? If you just experienced this too, your body just keeps functioning while you were traveling in other times. It's like real magic. With which you can also confuse.

The perception of time is a very manipulative area. Both in our own perception and in the perception of time epochs and time cycles. Both man and mankind can be controlled from the outside through active time regulation. However, the objective perception of time and history can raise many questions.

For example, we have managed to "invent" a Formula One car and supersonic airplanes within just 200 years from a horse-drawn carriage. Within 100 years, we went from quantum theory to the computer and even developed a powerful quantum computer.

But in the remaining 300,000 years[11] or even within 2000 years before our time, nothing, absolutely nothing decisive happened? Nothing except a few pyramids? How much manipulation is involved?

"Breathe" - "Did you notice the stork on the front page?"

---

[11] Human = "documented" for 300,000 years, Homo Sapiens, for "understanding, intelligent" or "wise, clever, intelligent, sensible human" according to Wikipedia. New archaeological finds prove that agricultural cultures already existed more than 1 million years ago.

The illusion of time has even greater effects.

The teachings of your ancestors, the children of Frya, were much wiser and more profound than we are led to believe. Here are just a few excerpts:

If there is no time, as your ancestors knew, your thought is the fastest thing that exists. And so what you have just thought has already been.

There is no here and now.

Nothing is now. Nothing is. Everything was.

As soon as you have thought this thought,
it is already in the past.
You can never think like that,
you have only thought.

All thoughts, actions and emotions that modern man deals with are already in the past the moment they happen. And yet they always bring back the suffering.

A plate that has shattered on the floor is already in the past. Why keep recreating it and getting angry that you weren't mindful? Even this thought is already past in your mind. So your ancestors taught children to increase their perception and mindfulness and to really perceive every moment. This is what reality means, from the word "work".

The reality[12] immediately becomes a different one. This means that all your fears are already in the past when you felt them, so everything is actually already over. Why hold on to it? This understanding is an important legacy from your ancestors.

"Take time to recognize the truth in it, because it can change your life and explain why your ancestors were so extraordinary and radiant."

"Seize the moment!" - Does that make sense?"

---

[12] Re-al-i-tät, Re-al-i-ty Re = "opposite of" - all - my - deeds.

There was only the beginning and the beginning, and they knew no end.

Since everything was and never is, everything is a beginning and so it only becomes when it begins. It never ends, but always has a new beginning. Like the circle or vortex[13] and the spirals within it. The basic principle of the cosmos or the law of conservation of energy. A cycle.

„WRALDA	T´ANFAG	T´BIJIN„
Warlda	The Beginning	The Start

Drawing according to Oera Linda[14]

Wralda, The Beginning, The Start These were the first three basic scientific principles, which were so important that they were immortalized on every tower that stood in the middle of the villages in Europe. These symbols can also be found in the Yule and stone circle.

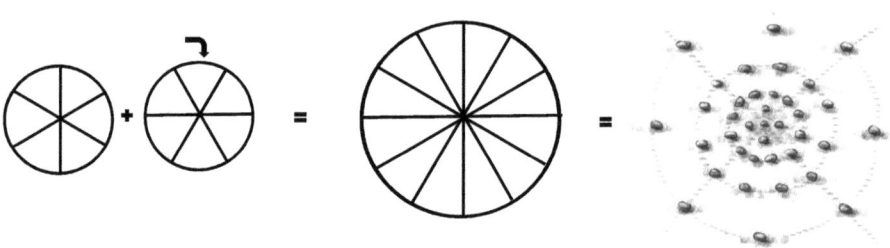

---

[13] Vortex - The cosmos, the earth, the human heart, the human body, all life is an electromagnetic energy system in the form of a vortex, an imaginary egg. Like the crown of the king's daughter (scene 1) and the chariot of faithful Henry (scene 12). The human heart is not a pump.

[14] The principles of Jul, the laws of nature.

But so much is denied and wrapped up in illusions. The Romans then twisted it again in their writings. Tacitus reports[15] (Roman historian) erroneously spoke of a "goddess" Tamfana who was worshipped instead of T'ANFAG.

„Germanicus[16] devastated a stretch of fifty miles with fire and sword. No age, no race found mercy. Profane and sacred sites, including those of those tribes (the Marsi[17]) highly famous temple, which they call the Shrine of Tamfana, was razed to the ground" Tacitus

They report proudly, completely naturally and quite openly about the extermination of your ancestors and even today they are still thoughtlessly glorified, honored and taught. Just like Alexander the Great, Julius Caesar[18] the Great or Emperor Charlemagne and many more. But people today no longer want to recognize it.

With the destruction of the tower, the basic knowledge and the most valuable knowledge of natural science of the highest growth and social cultures of several 10,000 years was simply wiped out.

---

[15] Publius Cornelius Tacitus (* around 58, † around 120) a Roman historian, politician and senator. Author of Germania (a twisted ethnographic writing about the "Germanic tribes") - "The victors write history".

[16] Nero Claudius Germanicus (* May 24, 15 BC; † October 10, 19 AD in Antioch on the Orontes) was a Roman general, known for his campaigns in Germania (Germanicus campaigns). He was the father of Caligula, grandfather of Nero and great-nephew of the first Roman emperor Augustus. An ancestral line and bloodline of mass murderers and liars. Quite naturally, glorified and honored in this world.

[17] The Marsi (Cherusci, children of Frya) settled in the Rhine, Ruhr and Lippe regions. They resisted the invasion attempts of the Romans for many centuries. Arminus (Hermann) the Cherukser, around 17 BC; † around 21 AD was, like many, abducted by the Romans as a child, trained as a "knight" with the oppressive and destructive spirit of Rome, only to return as a "prince". He recognized his true indigenous origins and pushed back the Romans at the Varus Battle. Until, 700 years later, Emperor Charlemagne had the last of Frya's children slaughtered and thus the Roman Catholic Empire held all free people captive to this day.

[18] Khazars, Caesars, Tsar, Khan, Emperor, Chancellor all have an identical root word that stands for a culture of domination and slavery.

Each hexagonal tower within the star fortresses and villages also had a "lamp" or fire (FODDIK), a place of education, science and truth. This lamp was the highest and most important asset of the Mothers of Honor and the tribes, to be protected at all costs. Every lamp in every village had to be "lit" at the primordial lamp in Texland, the seat of the Mother of Honor. Another important symbol of her wisdom and knowledge. It was more than just the sign of light as an all-animating being. She is so mysterious and mystical that there is certainly more to learn about her. If Odysseus himself wanted to light his light on it, as it is written. We can find further reports on this.

"They will bring their lamps and the light to light so that all people can see the truth. They will condemn the deeds of priests and princes."
From Oera Linda

So they report in great detail about your ancestors, here specifically about Buddha and Jesus. Who, like many other well-known names, were educated in the teachings of the indigenous European humanities[19] were. The knowledge of the highest principles of nature and ambassadors of the spirit of the children of Frya.

Picture left:
These are just some of your genetic ancestors. People with the spirit of the children of Frya. People of high conscience who left knowledge, prosperity, peace, justice and freedom all over the world. They did not seek followers but free thinkers. The "historians", priests, professors and rulers turned them into gods or saints, twisted and mutilated their teachings to maintain their own power and their true teachings were kept elitist. But their wisdom is still in your genes. You just have to remember.

From left to right:
Quetzalcoatl[20] (Kukulkan, Huiracocha), Deganawida, Jesus, Tyr (Wodin, Perun), Buddha, Hermes Trismegistos,
Apollonia von Alexandria, Iduna, Frigg, Frya, Minerva, Helena, u.v.a.

---

[19] Spirit = Spirit - Spirit refers to something that exists in a different "material" density - representing the invisible. Spiritual science or spirituality thus becomes evidence-based scientific wisdom about the electromagnetic connections and laws of the nature of everything, including the invisible.

[20] There are reports of these extraordinary people in all indigenous cultures. It is worth researching these stories and many more around the world.

Minerva and the cosmic egg

Why were your ancestors turned into gods and their teachings concealed by images and symbols? As an example of the spread of scientific knowledge, its true use and its transmission through your genetic ancestors, I present to you your ancestor Minerva. The origin of the name Minerva means: Min Erva, my heir.

I would like to tell you a story here that may give you a different understanding of history, your heritage, the festivals, the world of scientific knowledge and the truth about "gods".

The story is about a woman whose name was Minerva. Because of her wisdom, she was also called Nyhellenia ("she who gives new and bright advice") and later Hellena. Her symbol was a night owl, a sheepdog, and she always carried eggs with her "symbolically". She lived around 3644 years ago on the coast of Europe and was the mother of a castle on one of seven islands known as Valhalagrad[21] called. The seven islands are strung together like pearls about five to ten kilometers off the German coast in the North Sea: the East Frisian Islands. Another castle mother, nicknamed Kelta (The Cold One), with the coat of arms of a cockerel, lived near the Scheldt, a river that stretched from the Netherlands to France. Kelta was jealous of Minerva, as they wanted to make her the mother of honor of all Freya's children. Kelta sought advice from the hostile Magyars and sought support from the Gauls. They helped Kelta to make her people drunk, incite them and, with the help of the Gauls, attack Valhallagrad. Minerva now had to flee with her lamp and her people. She was rescued by Jon, a sea captain, and together they fled as far as the Mediterranean to Attica (Greece) and on to modern-day Athens (from Ata = the eight, the allies).

---

[21] In Norse mythology, Valhalla is the resting place of fighters who have fallen in battle and proved themselves to be brave, the so-called Einherjer. Or do the ancient scriptures, similar to the Mahabharata in India, refer to real personalities and the true "spirit" of their teachings? Ambassadors of the children of Frya? Valhalla, the Hall of Elections.

There in Athens in the 16th century BC in the heyday of the Bronze Age, she became known as Helen.

Text from the Oera Linda:
"When Nyhellenia, Hellenia, whose first name was Minerva, was firmly established in the country and the Greeks loved her almost as much as their own people, a group of princes and priests came to the city castle and asked Minerva where her "erva" (inheritance) lay. Hellenia replied:
"'Mina'-'erva' ('my inheritance') I carry in my breast. What I have inherited is the love of wisdom, justice and freedom. If I were to lose that, I would be like the meanest of your slaves. For now I like to give advice, but then I would sell it."

Once they came and asked: "So if you are not a sorceress, what is the purpose of the **eggs** you always have with you?" Minerva replied: **"These eggs are the symbol of Frya's advice, in which our future and that of all humanity lies hidden."** Time must hatch them and we must ensure that they are not harmed."

The priests replied: "Well said, but what about the **dog** on your right?" Hellenia replied: "Doesn't the shepherd have a sheepdog to keep his flock together? Like the dog in the service of the shepherd, I am in the service of Frya. I must watch over her flock."

"That does indeed make sense," said the priests. "But tell us, what does the **night owl** that always sits on your head mean? Is this light-shy creature perhaps the sign of your clairvoyance?"

"No," Hellenia replied. **"He helps me remember that a certain race of people roam the earth, who, just like him, make their homes in temples and caves and gnaw in the dark. Not like him, though, to help us get rid of mice and other pests, but rather to devise deceptions to rob other peoples of their knowledge so that they can seize them more easily, make them slaves and suck their blood like leeches."**
..from Oera Linda

The Hellenistic and Minoan cultures of Greece are among the most outstanding remnants of European civilizations. How is it that with the arrival of Helena in Athens, many "goddesses" with the attributes owl, egg and apple can be found throughout the area around the Mediterranean?

Minerva, New Hellenia, Hellenia, Germany - Owl - Egg - Shepherdess, castle mother of Wallhallagrad, candidate as honorary mother of the children of Freya.

Helena , Greece - Egg - Daughter of Zeus born from the egg, fought with three goddesses Hera, Aphrodite and Athena over the apple of Eris. "Conqueror" of the archons = rulers of Greece.

Athena, Athena, Atana Greece - owl - (Atana = the owl, bright-eyed, goddess of wisdom, strategy, combat, arts, crafts, manual labor, patron goddess and namesake of the city of Athens).

Minerva, Italy - owl - protector of craftsmen and trades, patron goddess of poets and teachers, goddess of wisdom, tactical warfare, art and shipbuilding and guardian of knowledge.

Ashtar, Astharte, Syria, Egypt, (Mesopotamia) - owl - eggs "The woman who made the towers", queen of heaven and goddess of love.

Iduna, Norse mythology - Apple, "Golden apple, the fruit of the tree of life", goddess of youth and immortality, the renewer, the rejuvenator.

Ishtar, Istar, Ashtaroth, Iraq (Babylon) - Owl - Eggs - ("The woman who made the surrounding wall.") - Goddess of desire, deity of war.

Ostara, Eostra, - Egg - Goddess of fertility and agriculture. Bringer of light.

Easter, Easter - egg - spring festival, festival of new life.

After Minerva left, the people were wiser and freer, but no priest or prince could use that, so they made her into one or even several goddesses and used, hid or distorted her teachings. What is it about the symbols (egg, owl, apple)? What can be found in their representation as the smallest common multiple? What is the cosmic egg?

The cosmic egg, the owl, the apple and electromagnetic fields

MIN ERVA - MEIN ERBE (MY HERITAGE)

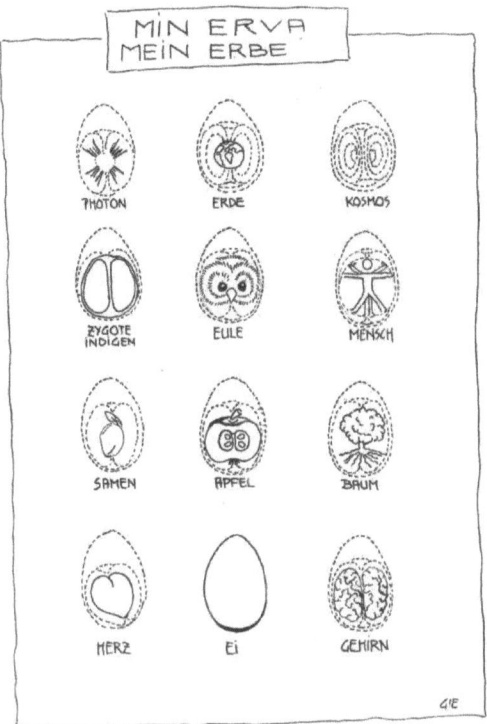

"*In the creation myths of many cultures and civilizations, the world egg (world egg) or world egg (also cosmic egg or Mundane egg) appears as a kind of beginning, during which the universe or a primordial being is created by "hatching" from the egg, which in some cosmogonic myths lies in the primordial waters of the earth. It symbolizes the absolute primordial state of the universe in the world creation legends of many Indo-European cultures, including the Indian, Greek, Persian and Baltic cultures. Outside the Indo-European language area, it occurs on the European continent in Finnish mythology, on the African continent in the ancient Egyptian hermopolitan cosmogony and in the mythologies of the Bambara and Dogon in Mali. In Asia, it is part of the mythology of the Dayak on Borneo and of Chinese and Japanese mythology, in Oceania it appears in Polynesian mythology and in North America in the mythology of the Cupeño in California.*

In the mythologies, the world egg corresponds to the absolute original state of the universe, from which a primordial being developed, which was often a twin or hermaphrodite, or which otherwise symbolized the union of two complementary principles." Quelle: Wikipedia 2024

Isn't it amazing how pictorially, scientifically[22] the ancient teachings were simple and clear? What else did your genetic ancestors know that has been suppressed to this day, but which today's science confirms time and again?

Indigenous cultures distinguish between knowledge and wisdom. So this simple example of your ancestor is only the beginning of a deeper understanding of this tale.

---

[22] Natural science as a combination of the understanding of spiritual (invisible, electromagnetic) and material knowledge. Which, when applied, leads to evidence and wisdom.

The golden ball

Light - Energy & Life - Conscience - Cycles - Energy wheel

The happy, free people of Frya, the king's daughter, lived in a golden, happy time. Because prosperity had nothing to do with matter. Prosperity began on the inside, with the feeling of freedom. The "golden ball" radiated out of them and connected with everything that was there.

The frog, the happy, joyful people, has lost the memory and the truth in it. The golden ball, also called the light of life[23], no longer shines so brightly in the depths of the well of time. But it still exists. If you are very attentive, you can even feel it. How every leaf, every tree, every blade of grass carries the same radiance. You can even see how this sphere makes you and all plants and animals grow.

---

[23] Light, photons (from the ancient Greek φῶς phōs "light"; singular "the photon"), also known as light quanta or light particles, are the energy "packets" that make up electromagnetic radiation. Physically, the photon is regarded as an exchange particle.

When time flies, you can watch how the biggest tree can grow from the smallest seed. From the inside out. It is like a golden ball or a golden sphere that surrounds your body with wonderful warmth. The indescribable, which has been given so many names.

A single secret key word that has many meanings, like the golden ball, can be found in the ancient scriptures. Rig[24] - the radiance that guides our lives. They spread the knowledge in all 4 cardinal directions. First in the north, where the knowledge is called the Vedas, in the east it is called the Vedas. But it was increasingly hidden and brought into secret. Today we may still know the Rigveda in the East, the Santia Vedas in the North.

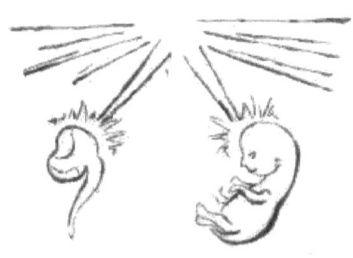

The children of Frya also knew the power of the invisible, it was called WRALDA, which is in us, the power of the invisible that connects us to the earth. They knew the power of the spirit and the elements, the power of nature, with which we are connected. The power that connects everything, like a spatial force. Wralda, the invisible nothingness, which is not nothing just because you don't see it, but which is everything because you feel it. It is not nothing, it is everything.

This is what we also call consciousness and life. As we find it in the North American medicine wheel, the counterpart to the Yule Wheel, in the Dao and Wu-Wei of Lao Tzu, the Bon of the true teachings in Nepal, the Zen of Shinto and even in New Zealand through Aotearoa. We find it in the sciences and teachings of the Siddhi of Yoga and Sidees (Túatha Dé Danann) of Ireland. All are based, like the knowledge of your ancestors, on a single source, natural science, the combination of spirit [spirit as quantization of electromagnetic radiation] and material science.

They used the intelligence, the knowledge of their bodies, the truth and secrets of the circle, the common space in which they lived, to make life fruitful and peaceful for everyone - from the inside out.

Your ancestors knew the laws of the world.
From the cosmically largest to the tiny smallest.

---

[24] Rig = ruler of the realm, king, Heimdahl (home - valley), Heinrich (grove - realm), Rig = light (R) is the gift, gift (G) of creation (I), guiding ray

Everything was centered on the circle.

They found the letters and runes in the circle. They saw life in the circle. They ordered time in the circle. The smallest building block in your body, the cell, is a circle. The order in the cell is in a circle. The earth is a circle. You find the universes in the circle. Who you are, that is the circle.

The happiness of all was their gold, the power that worked in them for all.

All this information is stored in the smallest components of your body, your genes. If you read on, you won't find anything new. But you will remember. You will feel it, you will know it. Everyone who is ready to get back on the old path will remember the essence and ancient knowledge of their ancestors and you will be the memory of your descendants. It is within you. It is called INDIGEN - In your genes.

The sphere also symbolizes the most precious gift of life, the CONSCIENCE, the genetic knowledge of nature and its harmonious principles.

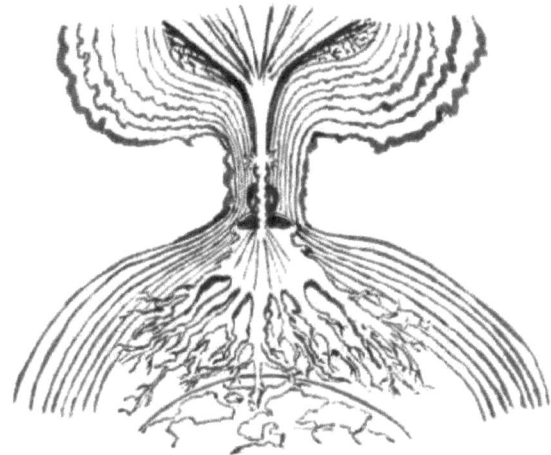

Throughout the ages, mankind has played with it, or rather allowed itself to be played with. It seems to be constantly losing its conscience, bringing fear, hunger and death. Today, mankind seems to be so bored with life that it loses itself in the flow of decay, oblivion and death through service-oriented work (work = Russian rabota - robot).

The golden age falls into the depths of the well - when times became darker. We know the call of the inner voice of conscience and the old, indigenous knowledge from many eras and times. Even today, this voice is getting louder and louder. Already 100 years ago, there was a similar voice that was heard by the European peoples, quietly and yet noticeably, just as many hear it today. A hundred years ago, it spoke of quantum mechanics, the Copenhagen interpretation of Niels Bor and Walter Heisenberg, of ecological life in Monte Veritá, yoga and shamanism, Viktor Schauberger's implosion energy, personality development and the psychology of C.G. Jung, the orgone energy of Wilhelm Wilhelm Schauberger, and the energy of the human body. Jung, orgone energy by Wilhelm Reich, mythology and mystery studies by Bülow, theosophy, anthroposophy by Steiner, electroculture, the secret of light by Walter Russel, free energy by Nikola Tesla, mesmerism, hypnosis, trance by Mesmer, ethics by Spinoza 200 years ago and, and, and. Europe has always been a cornucopia of knowledge in the humanities, natural sciences and cultural sciences. Or rather, memories.

Even today, people are returning to this tradition, unfortunately through other cultures from the East, West or South. Yet this knowledge also has a common origin in Europe. The free people and their life in the awareness of the circle brought abundance and freedom for centuries. They traveled to all coasts of the world to trade. Many peoples adopted their teachings. They are still talked about today in sagas, songs and legends all over the world. Because their shining eyes and their noble, aristocratic behavior had a special radiance.

This did not always please the princes and priests of the countries. Because they always had a free choice when it came to Frya's children. When they died or left, their values, knowledge, stories and legends remained. The princes and priests, however, used this circumstance to regain power and keep the people down. They turned the children into fryas, gods or idols. Religions, legends, myths, false philosophies and values were born and the dark times began.

You will eventually hear of Wodan and Odin, Inca and Thyr, Jesus and Moses, Mohammed and Buddha, Helena and Minerva, Ishtar and Astarte, Apollo and Apollonia, Hercules and Odysseus, Quetzalcoatl, Deganavida and many more all over the world. Of cities like Valhalla, Attica, Tunis, Athens, Avalon, Shamballa.

These are your ancestors, the Happy People, the children of Frya. Who have left peace, justice, freedom and knowledge all over the world.

But times got worse and catastrophes struck the earth again. The golden happiness, the circle and the communities fell to the ground. The ground became harder and other peoples kept coming to their land.

Just as they themselves always helped others in need, they also helped you. However, they did not return to their countries, but seduced the people as if in a whirlpool. They brought something with them that had previously been of no value to free people. Cunning and lies, power and powerlessness, faith and deception, distortion and division flooded the land.

Free people became slaves. No one was supposed to be equal, everyone was supposed to be better. Even today, this spirit of "being better" corrodes the childlike mind. Even today, fighting corrodes the aristocratic strength of children. Even today, illusions corrode the energy of children.

The class system took over the circle system. What used to mean equality among all became a class system, a separation of different classes, which still applies today, even if it is no longer so conspicuous. There used to be 4 groups, the merchants and sailors, the craftsmen and farmers, the sages and scholars and the warriors, who worked together cooperatively. Until today, the warriors (emperors/government) and the priests (magicians/scientists) took over the "good" of the general public.

It was the people who stood in a circle around the center. The center of the circle was the common fire, the common spirit, the common values. They served the common goal, the common life. These were the teachings of the old middle class. From this, princes and magicians created the class or caste culture, which has not changed to this day. A hierarchical culture that created different classes and castes like a pyramid or a triangle. Of gods, priests, princes and slaves. Of popes, emperors, feudal lords and peasants. Or of today's ruling, upper, middle and lower classes.

Like a virus, like a dark ulcer, the world changed into a dark, mendacious, violent, obedient, lawless, superstitious, transfigured, hypnotized culture of civilization right up to the present day. They brought Kronos - the god of time - into the country and he spread like a wild horde. Magicians spread illusions and call it marketing today. Warriors who wanted to be kings brought conquest and domination. Good men became gods, nature became fear. Wisdom became laws, the more laws, the less free people became.

They brought haunting and lies to the land. The magicians explained that there were evil spirits and promised that they could banish evil spirits. People's minds began to be haunted. You may still hear this haunting in your head today. As if they were still talking to you today, like judges, executioners, seducers, saviors, telling people about demons and gods. The illusion of darkness was perfect. Because people had forgotten to teach their children primal knowledge and indigenous natural science. Instead, they robbed the children, locked them in schools and inoculated them with incomplete, meaningless knowledge. This robbed the children of their time. In the past, children learned to think for themselves, set priorities and justify their views. In earlier times, they had achieved much greater intelligence through their own actions and the support of their elders. The magicians promised them a magical world. They promised them superhuman abilities that they had only forgotten, cures for diseases that had never existed before. The introduction of alcohol and nonsensical parties did the rest. Like a dark nothingness, a plague of wars, sacrifices and fear spread through all countries, which still captivates people today.

War brought the desire for war, or was it the other way around?
Fear brought narrowness of feeling. They twisted the language and the words that we still use thoughtlessly today because we have forgotten their origins. We continue to tell their stories thoughtlessly, of emperors and conquerors. Of religions and spirits that rule us. Of saviors and the supernatural who take responsibility away from us.

What was once a happy people has become a fearful people. Even today, people still speak contemptuously of a frosty nature. This is what the symbol of the frog also wants to express. Honest, truthful people did not know lies, only the truth of nature. That is why at some point they also believed the promises of magicians and princes. A virtue was turned into a weakness. A once strong, virtuous woman Tusnelda became a bimbo.

Everything was twisted:

"The honest man is the fool" The spoken word, the thought planted itself like a virus in people's minds. So you only hear "honest equals stupid". And a thought becomes a belief that is passed on from generation to generation. So nobody wants to be honest anymore, because then they are considered stupid.

Over the years, the nobles have fallen lower and lower. People forgot what they were really made of, that they shared and were their own master. That was the original meaning of "sharing" (= giving) and being master (ruling = being master)". So the princes and priests came, taught the people the stories of gods and demons, of science and culture. They spoke of fear and lack. Their aim was to "divide" the people and "rule" over them. The wisdom of mankind fell deeper and deeper into the well of oblivion. Knowledge was deliberately withheld from the people.

The last free people in Europe were generally referred to as Germanic tribes or Celts. But it was the Frisians and the Saxons who ultimately had to sacrifice either their lives or their freedom. Like all conquerors, the Romans (emperors) destroyed the forests, all knowledge and habitat was wiped out over many ages. The last children of Frya fought back until 700 years ago. Until a bishop (Boniface) cut down the last family tree and an emperor (Charlemagne) slew the last free people. The culture of war and sacrifice of darkness completely overshadowed the country.

In the Neverending Story by Michael Ende, this story is also told. The child princess - are the children of Frya the Bright. The Nothing, are the migrations and the wars, the culture of war and sacrifice of the caste pyramid, the extinction of the children of Frya and the circle culture up to the present day.

Humanity drops the golden ball of life down into the dark well of oblivion and has been fighting for ages with the dragons they themselves have let in.

The deeper it fell, the more people lost their common knowledge and their own conscience.

The inner voice, which always spoke virtuously and kindly to the people, split into a thousand splinters, became more and more divided, so that a few could rule over many. People's hearts had fallen deeply, becoming more and more like cold stone. They became more and more slaves on the outside and slaves to their passions.

And the croaking, moaning and complaining of humanity grew and grew until it could be heard all over the world. *Many religious books tell of coming saviors. In the writings of the Oera Linda, however, we can read:*

"Frya will return when we are free of all addictions and are no longer slaves! Hail to the free. They will see me again in the end. But I may only recognize as free those who are not slaves to others, nor to their own passions. The despondent will always succumb to their own suffering!"

If we understand the old legends again, you will find clues to your true origin in a few tiny pieces. It is not the parts of war, of rulers, of sorcerers, of envy, of hatred that you are attracted to. It is the small fragments of conscientiousness that you recognize. It's still in your genes. But as the world has become darker and darker over many millennia, all that your brain has ever perceived as truth is just the darkness of the world we grew up in. This darkness is stored in your brain as if you have been hypnotized for thousands of years. This is how the world has been shown to you and how this world has been kept small in you and around you. Like a mental artist, many generations have been distracted from its origin.

Now it is your time to take up your inheritance. You are an indigenous European, a European Native, a descendant of the free people of Europe, a child of Frya.

All the world's indigenous peoples are waiting for Europe.

The indigenous consciousness is the knowledge of your genetic heritage, the knowledge of the circle, the one ring, the crown of the Frog King.

The Frog King is, in truth, the initiation into this ancient knowledge and the way "to be aware of it". With every word and every syllable, with every image and every metaphor, it shows the way to regain the indigenous heritage. But it is also a hero's journey, because a change has to happen. You are not Indigenous until you come to terms with the knowledge of your genetic heritage. This is what Roman law suppressed.

It's up to you now. It is your journey. At the end of it, the faithful Heinrich awaits you. He is the "Heimdall" who leads you home to the sacred groves (Heiliger Hain) [25] of your ancestors.

---

[25] Sacred Grove (Hain): Don't be confused by the "official" interpretation. The sacred HAIN is: H - Cosmos, A - Ancestors, I - Creation, N - Knowledge "The place where your ancestors taught the knowledge of circular consciousness, creation and the cosmos" In the circle of the forest.

HUMAN LAW   COLONIALE   INDIGENT   NATURAL LAW

PYRAMIDAL CULTURE   # CIRCLE CULTURE

System-centered	ORIENTATION	Nature-centered
MAXIMUM YIELD	GOAL	FOR THE NEXT 7 GENERATIONS
EXPLUSIV - Consuming from the outside	IMPULSE	IMPULSIVE - GROWING FROM THE
CENTRAL	ORGANIZATION	INSIDE
SELECTIVELY	EDUCATION	DECENTRALIZED
FINALLY RESOURCE	ECONOMY	HOLISTIC - LIFELONG
RAIDING IDEAL	FINANCE	CYCLE | SUSTAINABLE
COLLECTING CONSUMPTION	ENERGY	FACTUAL | SHARING
3 FORCES	DEMOCRACY	PRESERVATION
THEORETICAL	SCIENCE	CONSENSUS
HIRARCHICAL	ORGANIZATION	NATURAL SCIENCE
DISSENT	COMMUNICATION	EQUALITY
SUBSISTENCE - Holding still	MEDICINE	HOMOGENEOUS - Uniform
SUBSTANCE CHANGE	NUTRITION	INHERENT
OUTSIDE THE MAIN	JUSTICE	NATURAL
CONCEPTIONALLY	TECHNOLOGY	INCLUSIONARY
MONOTHEISTIC	PHILOSOPHY	SUBORDINATE
CHANGE VALUES	THEOLOGY/RELIGION	NATURAL HOLISTIC
ENTERTAINMENT	ETHICS	TRADITIONAL VALUES
ENTERTAINED	ACTING	EDUCATIONAL
TREND	MUSIC	HARMONIOUS
PRESENTING	ART	NARRATIVE
INDIVIDUAL	DANCE	COMMUNITY
ANAEROBIC	MOVEMENT	AEROB

1. The origin of all circular and advanced civilizations, megalithic cultures, star fortresses,...

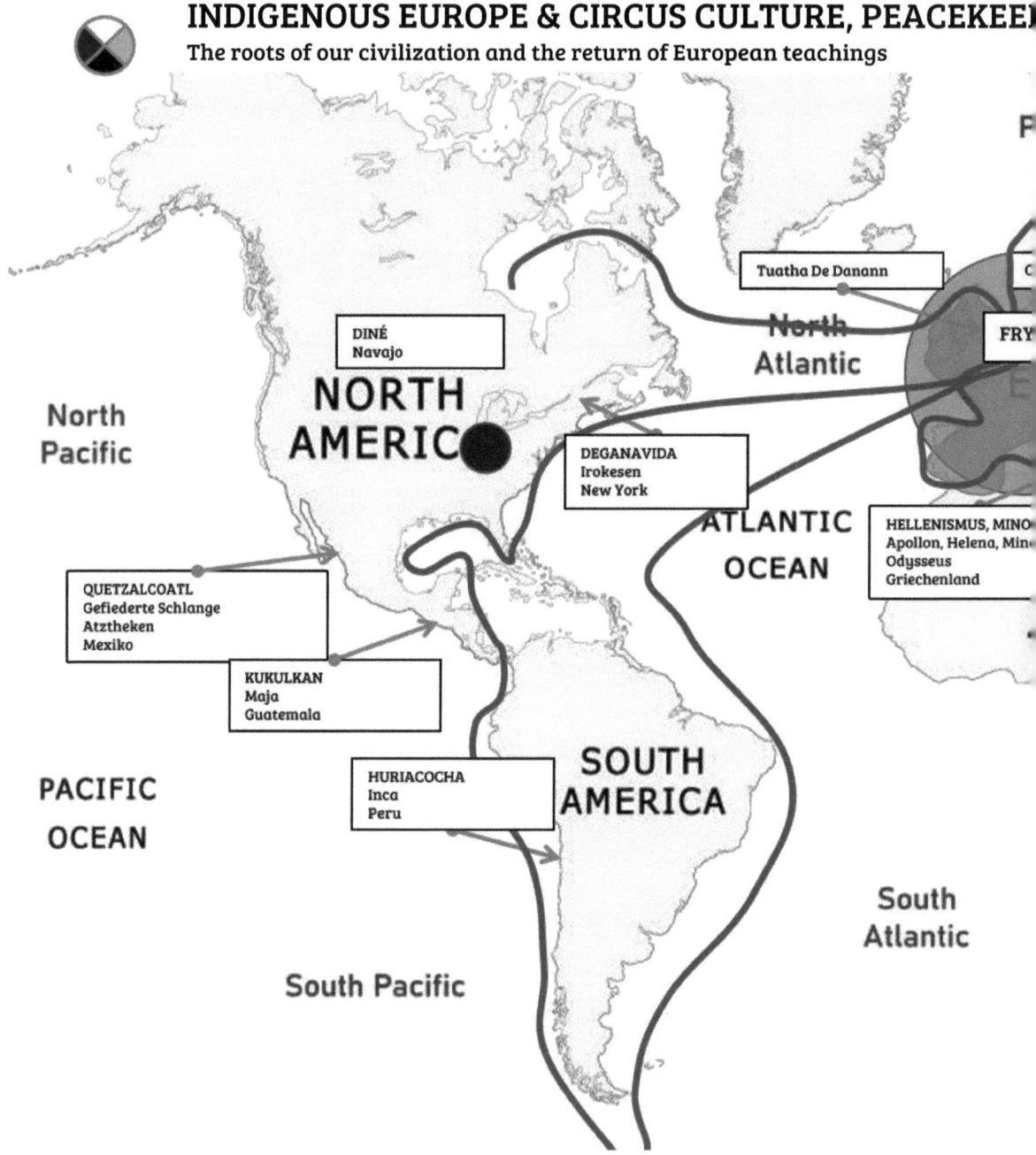

INDIGENOUS EUROPE & CIRCUS CULTURE, PEACEKEE
The roots of our civilization and the return of European teachings

Tuatha De Danann

North
Atlantic

FRY

DINÉ
Navajo

NORTH
AMERICA

North
Pacific

DEGANAVIDA
Irokesen
New York

ATLANTIC

OCEAN

HELLENISMUS, MINO
Apollon, Helena, Min
Odysseus
Griechenland

QUETZALCOATL
Gefiederte Schlange
Atztheken
Mexiko

KUKULKAN
Maja
Guatemala

HURIACOCHA
Inca
Peru

SOUTH
AMERICA

PACIFIC
OCEAN

South
Atlantic

South Pacific

2nd image, small. Map of every battle that has taken place since 2500 BC, according to Wikipedia (10,624 battles)

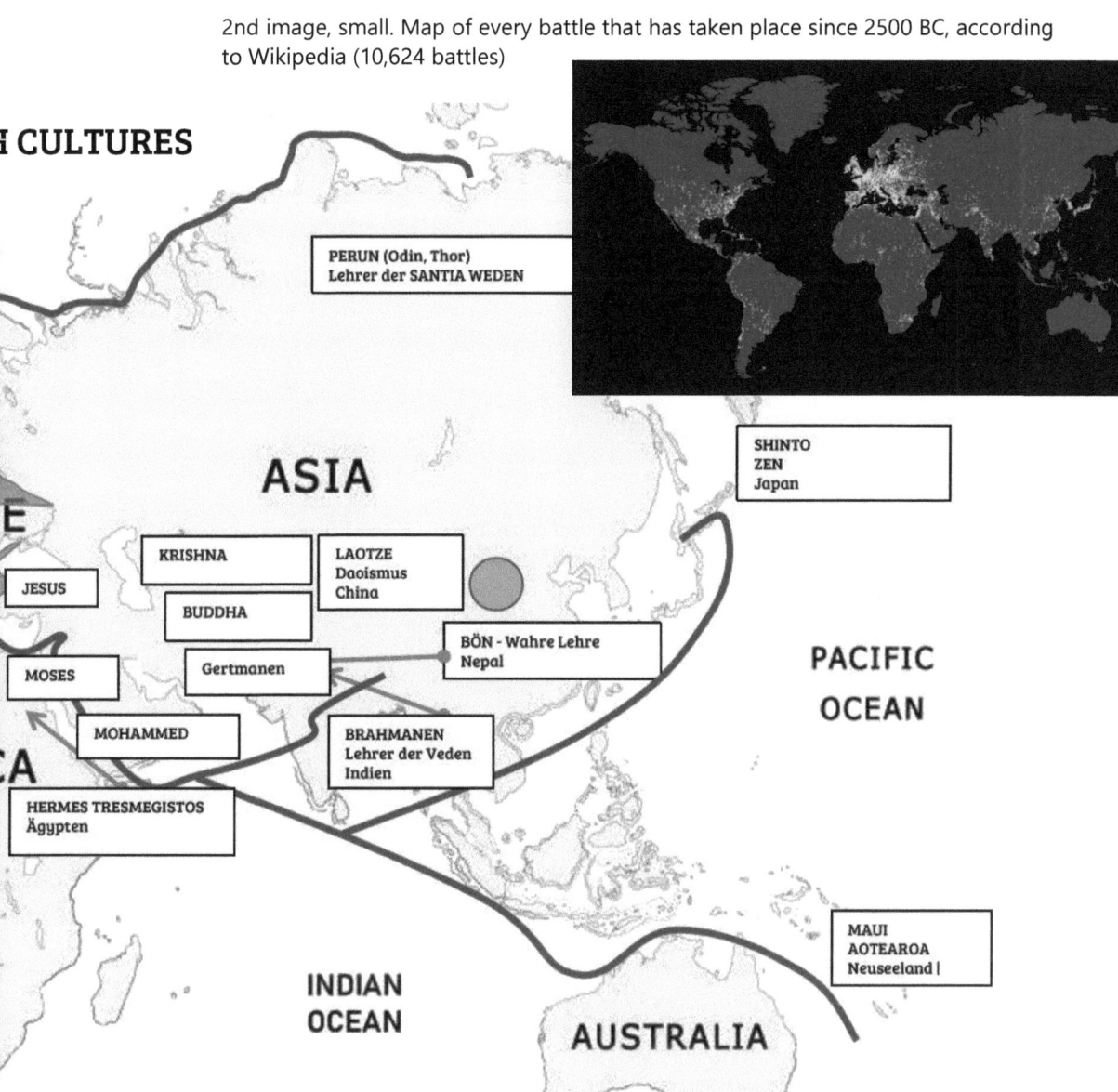

CULTURES

PERUN (Odin, Thor)
Lehrer der SANTIA WEDEN

SHINTO
ZEN
Japan

ASIA

KRISHNA

LAOTZE
Daoismus
China

JESUS

BUDDHA

BÖN - Wahre Lehre
Nepal

PACIFIC
OCEAN

MOSES

Gertmanen

MOHAMMED

BRAHMANEN
Lehrer der Veden
Indien

HERMES TRESMEGISTOS
Ägypten

MAUI
AOTEAROA
Neuseeland I

INDIAN
OCEAN

AUSTRALIA

EIDC.mittelstand.de
European Indigenous Developement Center
Europäisches Zentrum für Indigene Entwicklung

"A world full of goodness and conscience
is the earth for which every effort is worthwhile!"
Guido Eickhoff

The Frog King & the children of Frya

A message from your ancestors.

In [26] ancient times, when wishing still helped,

there lived a king whose daughters were all beautiful;

but the youngest was so beautiful that the sun itself,

which has seen so much, was astonished

whenever it shone in her face.

---

[26] The Frog King. Text based on the original by the Brothers Grimm. The Frog King or Iron Henry takes first place in the Brothers Grimm's Children's and Household Tales of 1812.

I

τλε INDIᎪᎬNOUS CONSCIOUSNESS

The indigenous consciousness - Cosmology

The awareness of the circle, the power of space and light, was the basic understanding of your ancestors. Everything begins with the circle, everything has cycles, everything is self-similar and everything is interconnected. This is the knowledge of ancient time. Everything is neutral and good in this everlasting ancient (ancient times) everything, the universe, which we now call the quantum field. The Ancient, the Primordial is the All, the Source, the Spirit, the Neutral, the Good. They called it Wralda.

They knew the "miracles" of the smallest elements of the cosmos, today we call them quanta, as neutral particles of light that interact with each other without time delay. The wondrous, timeless polarization and entanglement is the magic of this light, which ultimately becomes matter (wishes) and whose counterpart can be found in the vastness of the cosmos. This is the only magic that was pure natural science. It describes the process of our electro**MAG**net**IC** universe.

A ray of light (King= Rig)[27] passed through the darkness and created first space, then time and with it matter, a realm of abundance.

This is the cosmos (King)[28], the ruler of the realm and all matter in this realm is born from the "spirit" Wralda.

"Everything is created from the woman."(Daughters)[29], is the first sacred law of your ancestors. Every human being is born from a woman, she stands for life and the circle.

The union of light and matter also gives birth to all living things in this world. The earth, the plants, the animals and the people.

This cosmic light (King= Rig) is the electromagnetic energy.

It is the guiding ray- the Lord - who was conceived by everything and brought life. He channels life into the stars, the planets, the earth, the plants, the animals and humanity (Youngest).

You too are a royal child.

---

[27] King = Rig = The ray of light, the life, the life force, the life energy (Chi, Ki, Plasma, ...) and the guiding ray of life, the life energy in humans that guides life processes through health, illness, healing and much more.

[28] King = The cosmos determines all natural laws and principles. This is natural science. King = ruler of the realm, lord of the realm = (realm = abundance, treasure + lord = happy, ahd.) The "lord" of a realm makes the "realm" happy. (The principle of circle culture. The mothers/fathers of the peoples and tribes served with a clear conscience only as advisors to the people, not as decision-makers.)

[29] The mitochondrial genes are only passed on from mother to offspring. They form a network that extends throughout the entire cell. The mitochondria supply energy that is needed by the cell and are therefore the providers and connectors within the cell. Tribal life developed around the mothers of the people and mothers of honor according to this natural model. Decentralization is the secret of nature.

The sun (Sun) gives us this energy and it also shows us the cycles of the tides. Day and night, summer and winter and many other periods - these are the cycles of time. Humanity also developed in these cycles, it rose and fell again. People today would be surprised if they finally followed the true development of mankind.

Everything in the cosmos and on this earth, contains the spiral of life, the genetic (Face) Code. A tree becomes a tree, a flower becomes a flower and a person becomes a person. In this way, every life is given its own face. Everything is the same and yet each individual is different. This light information is stored in our genes and makes all of humanity indigenous [30].

That's why you too are Indigenous.

Using the example of the king, I would like to explain why it is so difficult to recognize the language of fairy tales. And why you find yourself in the well of a dream world. It is almost impossible to describe, which is why the true teaching was first experienced and then spoken. Images, synonyms and metaphors were used to make it easier to internalize the content, today it is called mnemonics.

What does it mean to be indigenous? You immediately have an image in your head. For example, you think of someone with a bow and arrow, poor, close to nature, etc. But this image has been shaped and deliberately implanted in people's minds and confirmed again and again on the outside in order to conceal the truth. But the reality is quite different. Look in the mirror and you will see a real indigenous, nature-born person. Nature-born also means being born in connection with your genetic connection to nature.

As another example, the word "apocalypse". Doesn't that make you think of the end of the world? But the truth behind the word means "unveiling", "revelation". So the Ragnarök, which we will get to know later, is also an "apocalypse" in images, but in truth it is a revelation. This manipulation technique is ancient and has been used since the Magyars. This is how the concealment of truth works. Unfortunately, this is no longer part of our children's education.

---

[30] Indigenous: ancient Greek: . Indi - Inner, Genius - Generate = created from within.

So what is the Frog King about?

It is about the human genetic heritage. It is about the scientific teachings and the associated attitude to life. It is the scientific understanding of light and life, of quanta and connection, of hidden knowledge and of your primal culture and the different interpretation of words. In order to "lift the veil now" [Another symbol from the Pistis Sophia (Greek: faith and wisdom), a Gnostic teaching. Which, like many other writings, such as Nag Hammadi scriptures, Bhagavad Gita, Bible, Koran, Talmud, ... or even today's science, do not really come close to the original core of knowledge, but with many words, veil more. The truth is always simple. It is evident, immediately obvious. So - electromagnetically - tangible], that also means "apocalypse", here is an example.

Nowadays, the word "king" alone creates a flood of information in your head, a trained and learned basic information that can be summarized as: "A king is the ruler of a kingdom". This is a self-evident meaning of the word king that has been repeated and confirmed since childhood. You know it from stories that have been told, from pictures, from history, perhaps you have often played it in your own mind and so on.

It is an association, a link in your brain with a certain idea. This is a common, unconsciously learned understanding of most people here in Europe, when they immediately project an image in their head with the word king. You may just see a throne, splendor, pomp, entourages, a castle, servants, estates and peasants.

In a world in which a child knows neither a "king", nor books or stories about one, nor the boundaries of the rich, nor even a demarcated land. Has no relation to the term rich for wealth, luxury, servitude, hierarchies or coercion. A child who cannot assign any meaning to the term "domination" because it does not know any images or experiences of one or more superiors. A child that does not grow up dogmatized, with fantasy concepts, but only with scientific contexts that it has experienced itself and that go beyond our "seven [31]" go beyond the meaning. Anyone who has grown up in such a world assigns a completely different meaning to terms such as empire and domination.

---

[31] We learn that there are only 5 senses. Seeing, hearing, smelling, tasting and feeling. Two crucial senses are not developed: The electrical and magnetic senses.

These terms also have a completely different meaning in Old High German. Here we find the terms abundance and treasure for the word "kingdom". In other words, a completely different image, a different feeling, a different train of thought. It refers to man himself, turned inwards and not outwards. On the one hand, it relates to the indigenous natural science of light and life and what we call quantum physics today. Through Wralda, you yourself are abundance and a treasure of elementary particles within you and around you, is this same neutral abundance and this treasure. Doesn't this bring a different feeling to life?

Secondly, this realm is everywhere, not just within you, but in everything on this earth and even more. So everything is connected to everything or a fractal aspect of everything. From stones to plants to entire planetary systems, this abundance is always there, in every moment.

How does a person who has grown up with this awareness and knowledge feel? Can you still feel "alone"? Incidentally, this is the true, former meaning of the word "all-one" - we are all one. But we have been implanted with the "feeling" of loneliness. Thus, in the original understanding and scientifically proven, you are connected to the entire cosmos and you yourself are an entire cosmos.

Our ancestors also had a deeper meaning for the word "Lord" than we have been led to believe. Your ancestors used it to mean being alive or being happy. Again, this is turned inwards. It is self-rule or self-control. Misunderstood by us as the doctrine of a "head". In our society, however, self-rule and self-control also have a completely different meaning. Here we know it more as pressure, coercion or torment. In the deeper consciousness of our ancestors, however, it means a feeling of freedom, vitality and joy. To be your own master, of your thoughts, your emotions, your life. In this way, you yourself become the king, the active, giving principle of life.

We don't ask ourselves: "What do I need?" -
We ask ourselves: "What can I give?"
(From the culture of the Iroquois)

This is the world in which Frya's children grew up and how it is still lived in some indigenous cultures. They were and are natural scientists and not half-savages.

So it is these two worlds that this fairy tale actually takes you into. And we try to put the world that you have observed as "normal" into a different perspective.

Close to the Castle of the king lay a great dark forest,

and in the forest under an old lime tree was a well.

Now when the day was quite hot, the king's child went out

into the forest and sat down at the edge of the cool well[32].

And when she was bored, she would take a golden[33] Ball[34],

threw it up in the air and caught it again.

And that was her favorite toy.

---

[32] Well = symbol for the stone circle.

[33] Gold = creation, positive life energy that enlivens every being with "energy/light", the rig ray.

[34] The sphere refers to the original teaching of cosmic life, from which all the teachings and natural sciences of this earth and its cultures have emerged. In the neutral wisdom of our ancestors, about the source of all knowledge and its teachings, we find the holy grail.

z

⊤∧ε ⊦ʀεε ρεορⅼε

The free people

A part of the humanity of this earth, lived in Europe, "your grandpa". Your noble ones lived there (noble = nobility) [35] Ancestors, ancestral ancestors and ancestors in the circle of their tribes. Later, they also lived in castles and fortresses that looked like poinsettias (Castle).

They were also called the "shining ones" (King/Rig)[36]. People with a clear conscience (con-science, **Shared knowledge**), the children of Frya who brought peace, the free. They were the descendants of the people of high knowledge and conscience who came from the north.

---

[35] Nobility: noble, conscientious

[36] King = rig, from Irish meaning ruler of the realm

They lived on the coasts and in the forests (forest) that covered the whole country.

Your ancestors were a gentle, peaceful people (Lime tree).
Everyone was equal, there were no kings, magicians or gods, there were no hierarchies.

They were the keepers of the knowledge of the stone circle (Wells)[37], the circular doctrine and culture, the source of all knowledge.(Wells1

But wars, conquerors and the forces of nature repeatedly swept across the earth(hot). Then mankind often sought advice from the peaceful people and their great knowledge. The children of Frya traveled in their ships along the coasts (Edge) of all the continents of the earth, trading there and bringing knowledge and peace. However, many princes and magicians did not like this because they wanted to enslave humanity. They were cold as ice (cool) and controlled the people who followed them. This darkness spread across the land until it completely overshadowed Europe. (Wells2)[38]

Many millennia ago (Long - while)mankind was still living in a much higher culture. This was the circle culture (Wells 1)the knowledge of the circle and the origin of all natural sciences on this earth and of cosmic life.

The principles of conscience (Ball2)[39], the common knowledge of the laws of nature, life (Kugel 1)[40], their forces and their cycles (Ball 3)[41].

---

[37] Well 1 - Mimir's (Giant) Well - Knowledge and Wisdom
[38] Well 2 - Nidhöggr (Dragon) Well - Knowledge and Consciousness
[39] Ball 2 - Circle culture - Conscience
[40] Ball 1 - Wheel of life - Life
[41] Ball 3 - Medicine wheel - Energy wheel

There was an age, a cycle (Ball4)[42]**, which today is called the "Golden Age". At that time, people knew about the power** (Ball3) **of space, of energy, of ether - they called it Wralda (the Urur-all-da). With which they, in harmony with nature, created natural positive values.** (Works) **made their hearts dance with joy** (Game = dance).

Throughout the world, we find the indigenous megalithic culture and stone circle culture over several ages, which, like the later star castle culture (Julburgen = Christmas star), were concealed in Europe. They also symbolize the indigenous matriarchal scientific circle culture.

Frya's children were the founders or influencers of all peaceful, highly civilized Wedic = knowledge cultures in all 4 cardinal directions. The Olmecs, Inca, Aztecs, Maya, Iroquois, Navajo in the West, the Vedas, Yoga, Dao in the East, the Hellenic and Minoan cultures and Hermeticism in the South, all the way to New Zealand. This means that all people and peoples on this earth are genetically connected with each other. It is a realm of communities of peoples with the earth from which you were born.

But the same game kept repeating itself. In retrospect, this positive development could not be suppressed or hidden. That is why individual indigenous Europeans were turned into gods. Faith cultures and religions were spread in this way. The perpetual strategy of "Magyars [43]"which is still causing nonsense today.

Confirmed, detailed records date back to 2192 BC, with some incredible details. Further information can be found beyond these ages. Which changes history as we are told it to this day, and which will have implications for our future.

Inland, this "land of peace" stretched from the North Sea to Tartaria, today's Russia. Tartaria is a land that also represents a hidden high-culture civilization with advanced technology from the 13th to 19th centuries, which has been confirmed by the opening of the official historical records of the current Russian president.

---

[42] Ball 4 - Wheel of Life - Cycles

[43] Magyars - An indigenous people from present-day Hungary. At that time, a synonym for an ethnic group from the Black Sea region, with Khazar values of usurpation and illusions.

Now it happened once,

that the golden ball of the king's daughter is not

fell into her little hand, which she had held aloft,

but hit the earthground

and rolled straight into the water.

The king's daughter followed her with her eyes,

but the ball disappeared and the well was deep,

so deep that you can't see ground .

3

ΤΛΣ DΣSCΣΝΤ Ο† ΜΛΝΚΙΝD

The descent of mankind

Humanity has played too often with the life of this earth and with its own life (golden ball). Mankind has always strived for more (...aloft), she became greedy, she wanted more and more from life.

This is how (...once), that around 4000 years ago, the earth once again experienced a cycle of catastrophes, causing the earth to shake. This led to migrations of peoples with many wars and conquests (hit Earthground). The old land, the Doggerland - today's North Sea, was a mainland that stretched from England to Denmark, the Netherlands and Germany, was flooded. This formed the coast of the North Sea as we know it today.

But their values, wisdom and laws remained.
The second sacred law was.

"Children are the most valuable asset to be protected."

"The first thing they taught their children was self-control; the other was the love of virtue, and when they came of age, they learned the value of freedom. For without freedom, all other virtues are good only to make you slaves, your origin to eternal shame." (Oera Linda)

They reflected on all their deeds and teachings until the seventh generation.

But humanity (King's daughter) watched (Eyes) like princes and Magyars, kings and priests, introduced class and belief systems. They promised them more prosperity and wealth, more security and rights, less hardship. As a result, more and more cultures of war and sacrifice sprang up all over the world like pyramids. The knowledge of the stone circles was buried under layers of mud. They turned the women and men who brought the knowledge into false "gods" and their teachings into false laws.

Conscience became less and less and times became darker and darker. Free people became slaves, slaves became fiefdoms, fiefdoms became citizens, citizens became staff (person-al) [44]. Like a dark void, the control of the few enveloped humanity. Conscience and free life (Ball) of every single person disappeared completely.

_____

[44] Person, lat. persona = mask

This fate (Wells 3) [45], has been repeated for many millennia and again and again over the last 4000 years. Up to the present day, the Golden Age has disappeared (golden ball) into the Silver Age, then into the Bronze Age and finally into the Darkest Age, the Iron Age, in which we now live. (Wells 3)

The incredible communal knowledge of the golden age fell into a hypnotic dark sleep of oblivion. All the old valuable knowledge was lost and where it was still to be found in libraries, they were reduced to their foundations (ground) burnt down.

---

[45] Well 3 - Fountain of Destiny - Urdbrunnen (Norse mythology) The Schick-sal - in the ahd (fate, holy order). In the word fate we find the original meaning as fate = human ability within the framework of a universal, sacred, healing = harmonious order. Those who recognize the knowledge of their own origin and the principles of nature attain dominion (=Swan = swans = pregnancy) over their own self-determined life.

Then she began to *weep* and wept louder and louder and
could not comfort herself at all. And how she wailed,
someone *called* out to her:
"What are you up to, king's daughter,
you're shouting that a *stone* would like to take *pity on.*"

She looked around to see where the voice was coming from and saw a
frog, who stuck his *fat, ugly* head out of the water.
"Oh, it's you, old *water puddler*," she said, "I'm crying over my golden
ball that fell down the well."

„Be *quiet* and don't cry," replied the frog,
"I can probably give *advice*, but what will you *give* me
if I bring up your toy again?"

"Whatever you want, dear frog," she said;
"my *dress*, my *pearls* and *precious stones*, even still
the *golden crown* that I wear."

4

τΛε ᏉUᎪᏒᎠIᎪNᏕ ᎧᏂ ᏟᏆᏕᎠᎧᎷ

The guardians of wisdom

The princes and magicians also brought the wine (cry) and generations of humanity fell deeper and deeper into intoxication, saddened by the loss of conscience and free life.

Although mankind still complains today, it has always heard an inner call, the voice of its own conscience (called), the call of its ancestors, the free man (frog).

She talks to us again and again. Why do people complain? True and honest joy has increasingly disappeared. Individuals do not understand that humanity is losing itself more and more in "bread and games" (...cry) and drunkenness.

The stones are the neurons of the universe (stones), our ancestors still knew that. They were lost more and more over time and so intelligence was inherited less and less (pity one). The heritage of the once happy people became more and more impoverished.

It was often a single person (frog) who came to the rescue and appealed to people's conscience. The indigenous peoples are the last guardians of this wisdom (water) [46]. But mankind mocks (fat, ugly) them. But they are the real teachers of science (water puddler).

Go into stillness (quiet) and listen to your conscience and stop drowning in sorrow (weeping) is the advice to us. We can make it if you reinstate the old advice (advice). The council of the common eight (respected women and men who live only for the community) that every tribe had. The tribal cultures that were free offer their help again and again.

Humanity should learn to give (give) again. The gift was the happiness of your ancestors - their children were encouraged in this. Giving and sharing what is valuable was their value system, which does not behave like a host. Giving was what brought happiness. Because they knew that if each individual was happy, then there would be an even happier whole.
Aber...

As humanity has learned over generations - from false magicians - it wanted to buy his services. For material goods created through much suffering (dress), through exploitation of the earth (gemstone) and exploitation of the seas (pearls). Humanity is even prepared to sacrifice its own power (crown), just like generations before it.

[46] Water is an information carrier.

Guardian of wisdom or magician

"Know thyself" - "temet nosce" . The call to understand the genetic creation, the laws of nature and of being human. This is what our ancestors, in Hellenistic antiquity [47] and was only taught in mystery schools. It was natural that the first step towards personal maturity was expressed in the aphorism. "You are nature".

"You are nature". This is the essence of natural science. This is the gift of the guardians of wisdom in a true society. In german the prefix "Ge[48]" (Ge-sellschaft = society, Ge-winn=profit) is what expresses the momentary event that denotes either the beginning or the completion of a process (give birth, give birth, prosper, please, belong, succeed, recover, happen, confess, grant, gain, accustom). The word "Gesellschaft =society" is about the unconditional gifts that we gladly share. It is a human gift to steer this purposefully. Because this means growth and the release of energy. From within, the light particles in our body then begin to radiate in waves; if we focus our attention on something, it becomes a beam (see double slit experiment). We then emit part of our energy into the environment. This gift made our ancestors "radiants" and this is how scientific magic worked.

The word magician (germ.: Magier) contains the opposite.
The Ma-Gier means Magnetic greed. If something is "magical", we seem to be attracted to it. There are many people who exploit this. Some consciously, some unconsciously. When we follow idols, when we worship something, when we give attention to something that seems to give us brief pleasure. When we go to meetings and the speakers get our attention. In school, university, church, parliaments, classes, in the smallest group, the speakers are front and center and all the attention is focused on them. In this way, we give our lives to someone else who magnetically absorbs them. In this way, they become the energy-following realms (successful). And the others become energy-followers (unsuccessful).

The teachings and thinking of our ancestors took place in a circle. As guardians of wisdom, those with the higher gift, the knowledge of all the connections, they were always part of the circle. This enabled them to pass on their gift, their knowledge and their energy to others. This creates a communal connection. The neutral fire in the center is the "soul" of the circle.

This is where we find our companions.

---

[47] "Know thyself" - "temet nosce" - Wisdom of Socrates and the Oracle of Delphi

[48] Ge = G-gift+ E-energy

The frog replied:

"Your clothes, your pearls and precious stones and your golden

crown, I don't like them: but if you want to love me,

and I shall be your companion and playmate,

sit next to you at your little table,

eat from your golden plate,

drink from your little cup,

sleep in your little bed:

if you promise me that,

I will go down and

and bring you back the golden ball." –

"Oh yes," she said, "I promise you anything you want,

if you just bring me the ball back."

But she thought: What a simple-minded frog!

It sits in the water with its own kind and croaks

and can be no man's companion.

5

TΛε ςεcρετ οʄ βειΝα ʌuмΑΝ - TΛε αεςειι

The secret of being human - The Companion (Gesell)

Conscience (golden ball) cannot be attained through material goods. The golden age will not awaken through this either.
Man speaks of the longing for love. (To have love).

Man was the Frosk (frog), a happy race, of a happy nature. But what was once a noble people has now become a frog nature.

The frog nature is fearful. Out of fear we let ourselves be led, out of fear we become angry, out of fear we become mean, out of fear we let ourselves be controlled, out of fear so much happens in the world that pulls us deeper and deeper.

Over all this time, people have forgotten what life means. They have allowed themselves to be dragged down more and more by the magicians and princes. Wealth, prosperity and appearance have become more and more important.

But deep inside every human being, there is this one voice. This one constant croaking. Everyone just wants to be loved for who they are. That is what the most ancient nature wants to tell us. When people realize again that all the luxury they seek and all the lack they experience only comes from the fact that they are no longer connected to themselves and to others. The search on the outside is a distortion.

„Having LOVE" - The mission
The word "love" (german: „lieb") is composed as follows in the sounds of the possible original language.

L = law of nature
I = Creation
E = human being
B = Questions

"You should ask yourself questions about being human, the laws of nature and creation."

If you can answer these questions, nothing is missing.

Conscience constantly reminds you to be aware of this. That is your mission. That is the reason for life, to recognize the connection to everything. We were not taught this in our childhood. But the genes, the library of life, the knowledge of your ancestors, call for it. Like a permanent call, every person can hear it within themselves. Why am I here?

This is the resolution to the meaning of life. The call for an understanding of genetic creation, the laws of nature and of being human. That was the first thing Frya's children were taught.

For the mystical philosophers of antiquity, it was self-evident that the first step towards personal maturity could be expressed in the aphorism: "Know thyself." For them, educating a person was the first step, achieving an inward spiritual focus so that he learns what is within himself. Before he tried to approach the outside world. They rightly assumed that he could not effectively assess and cope with the world until he fully understood his personal psychological and natural balance.

The table, the plate, the cup, the bed, the companion.
These images are deceptive. They seem to want to convey that humans (frogs) need nothing more to live than to satisfy the most basic needs. These attributes (eating, drinking, sleeping, ...) are the lower instincts of the reptilian brain (dragon).

The human brain stem, also known as the reptilian brain, acts completely autonomously and is only responsible for the survival of the body. This is part of the illusion used to keep humanity in fear. The battle with the dragon, the reptilian brain, is the key that we also find in the old trainings and in the legend of Siegfried with the dragon.

The true magic of life lies in the deeper meaning of the images.

There are five passwords that we should understand. We find them in the ancient mystery schools, which have their knowledge from the teachings of the indigenous peoples. The ancient knowledge, parts of which can still be found in all four directions.

The table, the plate, the cup, the bed, the companion

These are the 5 elements [49] of earthly existence:

Father, mother, creation, child becomes family

They are the 1, the 2, the 3, the 4 and the 5

They are the 5 primal elements: Fire, Earth, Water, Air, Ether/Wralda

They are the 5 elements of the energy wheel/medicine wheel of life

These are the 5 elements of life:
Body, mind, soul, emotion and community

---

[49] However, there is also an example of this in the Vedas of Asia:

In the Indian Vedas (Vedas = knowledge) they stand for a higher understanding of energy.

1. spirit man (Atma), 2. life spirit (Buddi), 3. spirit itself (Manna), 4. self.

Here it should be made clear that through the connection as spirit man (male principle, giving, electric or breath) with our life spirit (female principle, receiving, magnetic or body) only our spirit itself is created (through polarity, connection), which we call our self (4 matter). Unfortunately, something crucial has also been "forgotten" here in a "magical" way. The 5th, the totality and connection with all spirit. The invisible connections to all cosmic events.

In quantum physics we also find this principle: there is a neutral quantum field = 0 (everything, primordial universe), which can only be created through the entanglement (3) of two neutral quanta, which are polarized differently (1 and 2) without time delay over billions of kilometers, whereby matter = neutron/electron (4) can arise. These are the laws of nature and creation. These are the principles with which the children of our ancestors grew up. If you imagine looking at the world with this knowledge, how would humanity develop?

These are the 5 fingers of the hand that are connected to the carpus. No finger must be missing for success. The roots are your ancestors. And much more knowledge.

It is the lost knowledge and values of your ancestors.
This is where the magic of the bright, shining people, the heritage in your genes, begins. It was guarded for many ages, but mankind despised it and their lives became more and more locked up.

The shining conscience and truth (golden ball) has fallen into the darkness of lies and deceit. The indigenous peoples (simple-minded) and their matriarchal, birthing circle consciousness are ridiculed and their way of life is considered simple-minded.

However, humanity exploits their knowledge and thus began the marginalization, persecution and extermination of entire peoples. The children are abducted, re-educated, indoctrinated and turned into collaborators.

This is exactly what happened to your ancestors, the children of Frya, the indigenous people of Europe. The children (of his kind) in Europe were also robbed and re-educated, just as it still happens (promises to happen) today under the guise of early education and compulsory schooling. Only here, the centuries-long destruction began much earlier. 2000 to 3000 years under the rule of usurpers and magicians make us forget many things.

Darkness, war, destruction, jealousy, envy, false beliefs have completely darkened the earth and increased the torment (quakt).

The frog, when he had received the promise,

dipped his head under the water, sank down,

and after a while he came up again,

had the ball in his mouth and threw it into the grass.

The king's daughter was full of joy,

when she saw her beautiful toy again,

picked it up and jumped away with it.

"Wait, wait," cried the frog, "take me with you,

I can't run like you!"

But what good did it do him that he shouted his quack,

quack after her as loud as he could!

She didn't listen, hurried home and soon forgot about the poor frog,

who had to go back down into his well.

6

Τ Λ ε ς ε c κ ε τ ο ϯ Λ υ μ λ ν ι τ

The secret of humanity - the indigenous European circular culture

Seduced by the mendacious humanity that has developed in the meantime, individual people - the guardians of wisdom - trusted the promised word. They passed on their knowledge, which was then again misused only to maintain power.

Knowledge was always passed on orally (Mouth [50]) because otherwise it could not be experienced and understood.

Individuals wrote the principles of life in books (Grass = Linen [51]) down. To this day, mankind thinks that it is now once again the owner of knowledge, and flees from the true responsibility to fathom it more deeply (Jumped away).

---

[50] Script - The headings used here are in the 4000 year old "original standing script". It originated from the Julrad. There was also a so-called "Runschrift", which is still very reminiscent of the old German Sütterlin script. Source: https://oeralinda.org/en/product/fryas-standskrift-font/, https://wiki.oeralinda.org/view/En_06_Yule,_Script,_Numbers

[51] Linen - paper made from linen was the largest and most important commodity in Europe 4000 years ago.

The indigenous peoples repeatedly draw attention to the fact that life takes place together on earth and warn that the development of humanity is progressing (running) too fast and without consideration.

But on the contrary, they are being subjected to the agony (quack) of genocide. Just as here in Europe the indigenous source knowledge and our true ancestors are eventually wiped out by the Roman emperors and the Catholic priests.

The people of Europe ultimately forgot their origins completely and allowed themselves to be seduced. In this way, they have helped to spread the nothingness, the dark ages, like a black plague throughout the world.

And so the indigenous peoples of Europe and the true natural sciences of the former advanced civilizations fall into the sleep (well) of oblivion again and again.

Everything in this cosmos has a certain system. Coincidences are unnatural. Why should it be called natural laws if you can't find any regularities in them? The indigenous natural sciences have been dealing with the laws of nature, or perhaps better natural principles, for thousands of years, because they are evidence-based (evidence = immediate and complete insight, clarity, certainty). They are the origin of all sciences and teachings on this earth. Their models are the forest, the human body, cosmology, etc., just as we find them hidden in this fairy tale.

Individuals have dived down again and again and researched their genetic origins. But if they wanted to pass on too much, they had to go underground. Plato is a good example here. One of the greatest role models of Western philosophy, he talked about Hyperborea, Atlantis and the cave allegory. But this was already too much and he had to die. Pythagoras, another initiate, was actually a natural scientist, but his knowledge and teachings were reduced to a mathematical formula. (Can you hear them yet?) Leonardo da Vinci, Antonio Gaudi, Goethe, Wagner, there are so many names.

But almost all of them have 7 years missing from their CV. It's as if they were looking for something and then returned to publish groundbreaking wisdom, inventions, masterpieces like lighthouses. We can only read about them in books. The true masters of the unifying natural sciences of the circle have disappeared, the teachings have been divided into physics, chemistry, mathematics, philosophy, economics, democracy, art, music, theater, sports and, and, and ... The connection to the origin of the science of nature has been completely severed.

If a child is the first to understand the world and the universe, it will understand and LOVE the laws of all of nature. What deeds is it capable of when it understands this? But it cannot be read, it must be experienced, understood. That was the old doctrine of nature. If they are taught the laws of nature, which they can comprehend with their seven senses, they will develop an undreamt-of potential. The seven senses, of which only five are taught, trained or recognized today (seeing, hearing, smelling, tasting, feeling) have been restricted. The two crucial ones, the "electrical" and "magnetic" senses, which we find represented in the true connection between the brain (electrical) and the heart (magnetic), were elementary abilities that were part of a child's education. These are slowly being rediscovered by the new sciences.

The next day, when they were with the *king* and

all the *courtiers* had sat down to the *table* and

ate from her *golden plate*,

there came, splash, splash, splash,

something crawled up the *marble staircase*,

and when it reached the top,

it knocked on the door and called out:

"King's daughter, youngest, open up for me!"

She ran and wanted to see who was outside,

But when she opened the door, the frog was sitting in front of it.

Then she hastily threw the *door* shut,

sat down at the *table* again, and

she was terrified.

7

THε CONSCIOUSNεSS οf MΛN

The consciousness of people - The hero's journey

Even in the caste or class society **(king)** that still exists today, a few serve themselves at the table that is prepared by many. Humanity gave up its humanity and freedom in order to live like kings. The "middle class" **(courtiers)** pays court to the new princes and priests or slips down into the lower class. Church, economy, politics and many more feast on the living **(golden)** children **(plate = child)**, who are forced into this system at the earliest age (today already at three).

Rising deep from the well of oblivion/fate, individuals have (splash splash) made their way to their heritage.

To the table of their ancestors where all were equal. Every single person must recognize that their place is there. He too is a royal child, a Rig child, of the shining ancestors.

As a result, more and more people are rediscovering the old indigenous teachings and coming together more and more. People need to talk to each other openly again.

They have recognized their path (stairs) and are now on a mission (marble)[52]. These people want to find their self-confidence and lead a long and self-determined life. They just need to know that the only way is back to their origins. To the table and the source of their ancestors and their values. *"Your own path is only good if it serves everyone. The path is always for the good of the people."*

It's in your genes. It calls in your conscience. It is the call of your indigenous ancestors and their legacy that you will take up. You are the frog.

Now it is up to you to climb the path out of oblivion and go to the table of your ancestors. The staircase is the ladder of your genes, which contain all the information of all generations and all worlds.

---

[52] **M-AMOR:** M = man, Amor, Latin for love, backwards ROMA. Sounds like a magic word for the love of Rome. Please don't misunderstand.

MARMOR = Mission - formed from the runes: "When man speaks to man again about his heritage, his homeland, a new journey towards unity begins." Guido Eickhoff

It is Jacob's ladder that connects spirit and matter, a hero's journey. Your path (staircase) is for your good and your mission (marble) [53] *is for the good of others.*

But humanity, out of ignorance, is afraid of this. It has forgotten to stand up for its freedom (door) **and to identify itself again as indigenous Europeans. Otherwise it believes it will lose everything. The table is also the cross, the religion, the male fire, the patriarchy and the fork in the road, the decision, the responsibility. She must conquer her fear of self-responsibility.**

Your hero's journey:

"Always look ahead.
You can see your way there,
and if you do that, then you can accept your mission.
You choose the path that belongs to you, and the Creator will show you your mission.

Your mission is always for the good of people.
If it is not for the benefit of people and creation,
then it is not from the Creator. It is not your mission,
and you should re-examine your path.

Your path is for your good and your mission is for the good of others."
The Message of Tadodaho Chief Leon Shenandoah
(Grandfather and teacher von Thomas Arculeo, White Eagle)

---

[53] Mamor: MARMOR & Mutabor (similar sound values)
The central magic word in the fairy tale "Kalif Storch (Odbar, Adebar)" by Wilhelm Hauff is "Mut-a-bor". From the Latin it means: "I will be transformed." = foreign determination
But in our "original language": Mut-a-bor = MUT-IST-GEBOREN COURAGE-IS-BORN
Pay attention to which magician you follow. The power in our original language is much more precise and more and more, one recognizes the goal of the twisting of languages.

The *king* saw that her heart was *beating* violently, and said:
"My child, what are you afraid of, is there a *giant* at the door to take
you away?" - "Oh no," she replied, "it's not a giant, but a nasty frog." -
"What does the frog want from you?" –

"Oh, dear father, when I was sitting and playing in the forest by the
well yesterday, my golden ball fell into the water. And because I was
crying so much, the frog brought it up again, and because he really
wanted it, I promised him that he would become my companion. But I
never thought he would be able to get out of his *water*. Now he is
outside and wants to come in to me."

And then it *knocked* for the second time and called out:
"King's daughter, youngest, *open the door*,
don't you know what you said to me yesterday?
You said to me by the cool fountain of water?
King's daughter, youngest, open the door for me!"

Then the *king* said, "What you have *promised*, you must keep; go
ahead and open the door for him."

8

TʌƐ TURN Oʄ MʌN

The turn of man - The promise

Some people in business, politics and education (King), recognize very well the potential of a single person with indigenous knowledge (Giant) and call on them to identify themselves as indigenous.

But most people believe that the laws of man should be above the laws of nature. Humanity begins to make excuses again and again. They do not recognize the giant within them and they hope that the knowledge of their past (water) [54] because it would then have to give up its supposed security.

---

[54] "Returned" was used as a word to make it work again. The word returned sweeps it under the carpet again. We should try to pay more attention to the meaning of words and their sound again.

It has often been isolated people who brought people together, who knocked (knocked) on the gates of castles. The original sound could also be reminiscent of kloppen = to beat up and thus conveys images of incited and staged revolutions, civil wars and demonstrations. Too often, people thought that revolutions and wars would bring about change. But the consequences were even more suffering and the situation was not really changed.

But the frog, the happy, peaceful human being (after his hero's journey) and the indigenous peoples, your ancestors, keep knocking and asking (open up = wake up [55]) to wake up humanity. The "klopfen" in Old High German means to drum, to beat lightly, to wear down. They are the peaceful warriors.

But just like Cassandra[56], they are rejected. Humanity is afraid of the messages they spread. When they speak of Mother Earth and bring the truth to light. They are afraid of the immense greatness that has been declared to them when they achieve this freedom. Because freedom also entails responsibility. This responsibility often made it so difficult for humanity to stand up for itself again. All too often, they slammed the doors shut again. They don't want to know about any of this.

At this moment, the ancestors (king/rig) have their say.
It is about justice (promised) and right.

The human right.

---

[55] In the context of the word and letter twists, the M becomes a W. And the meaning becomes clear.

[56] Cassandra: Had the gift of visions and prophecies. But people don't believe her.

The prophecy of the 7th fire of the Anishinaabe *(North America, Canada).*

"Combining the material knowledge of the West with the spiritual wisdom and values of the indigenous peoples of this land is a path of healing and survival for all humanity."

"This time the light-skinned race has a choice of two roads. One road will be green and lush and very welcoming. The other road will be black and charred, and if they walk on it, they will cut their feet.

In the prophecy, the people decide not to take either path, - but to turn back to remember and regain the wisdom of those who came before them. -

If they choose the right path, the seventh fire, the eighth and final fire will be lit, an eternal fire of peace, love, brotherhood and sisterhood. If the light-skinned race chooses the wrong path, the destruction they brought with them when they came to this land will come back to them and cause much suffering and death to all people on earth."

The promise - "What you promise, you must keep."

"Your grandpa" - Europe (king/cosmos) speaks to humanity. The ancestors of the free peoples of Europe, people of conscience, keep reminding us of these times. The call of conscience. They remind us that we should keep the promise of past generations. To remind us again of the true values/laws of life. We return to the wisdom, the joyful people, the circle, the circle culture and the truth and the connection with everything.

When man reclaims the right of his ancestors.

The human right.

Many generations have lived in this system. They have participated, served, not moved. We still know the history of this time cycle. After the Romans wiped out the last free primitive peoples of Europe, the next generations were dragged into darkness.

After 700 years, the next darkness spread from Europe to the whole world. To spread the dark age there too. The spirit of the children of Frya, the conscience, was more and more extinguished. In the name of the kings and emperors and the new magicians/priests of the church, America, Asia and Africa were "conquered" - "civilized" - from the 14th century onwards.

Three papal bulls were written legitimizing the next genocide and the Vatican's [57] possession of the earth .

They symbolize 3 crowns

1st crown 1302 - UNAM SANCTAM - "A holy church"
2nd crown 1455 - ROMANUS PONTIFEX - "Doctrine of Discovery" - "The salvation of all"
3rd crown 1481 - AETERNI REGIS - "Eternal possession of the ruler"

This is not a fairy tale or a dream or a fantasy.
This is the law. Worldwide.

When major European powers tried to divide up the world among themselves in the 15th and 16th centuries, they relied on papal decrees. They have all remained in force to this day. Unfortunately, this is often forgotten.

The papal bull ROMANUS PONTIFEX "Doctrine of Discovery" contained therein was only dissolved on March 30, 2023.

It is now like a reversal, the redemption of all the people of these usurped lands. The right has been returned to the people.

---

[57] VATIKAN = Vat (Father, Vaner) i-st - Kan (Emperor, Caesar)

The promise or the debt [58]

Our own history and that of our ancestors has been burdened with guilt, a guilt that is stored in our genes.

A debt is also a promise.

So the now fearful people are very easy to direct. But the connection to our ancestors, the return to our indigenous culture and the union with the indigenous cultures of this world, can bring about the true path to a better future. They are reaching out to us.

We just have to take it and fulfill the promise of our ancestors.

If we reconnect the indigenous natural sciences (spiritual/spiritual wisdom) with today's acquired material (material knowledge/realization, implementation) knowledge, we can experience another sustainable and peaceful cultural evolution. It is up to us to seize the opportunity.

You create your own life yourself and constantly.

Why not this world?

---

[58] At the Urdbrunen, the Fountain of Fate, three Norns weave the web of life.
Cause/past (Urd) becomes effect/present (Verdandi) becomes guilt/future (Skuld)

"The fate of your life is only in your hands. It is your debt (=promise)."

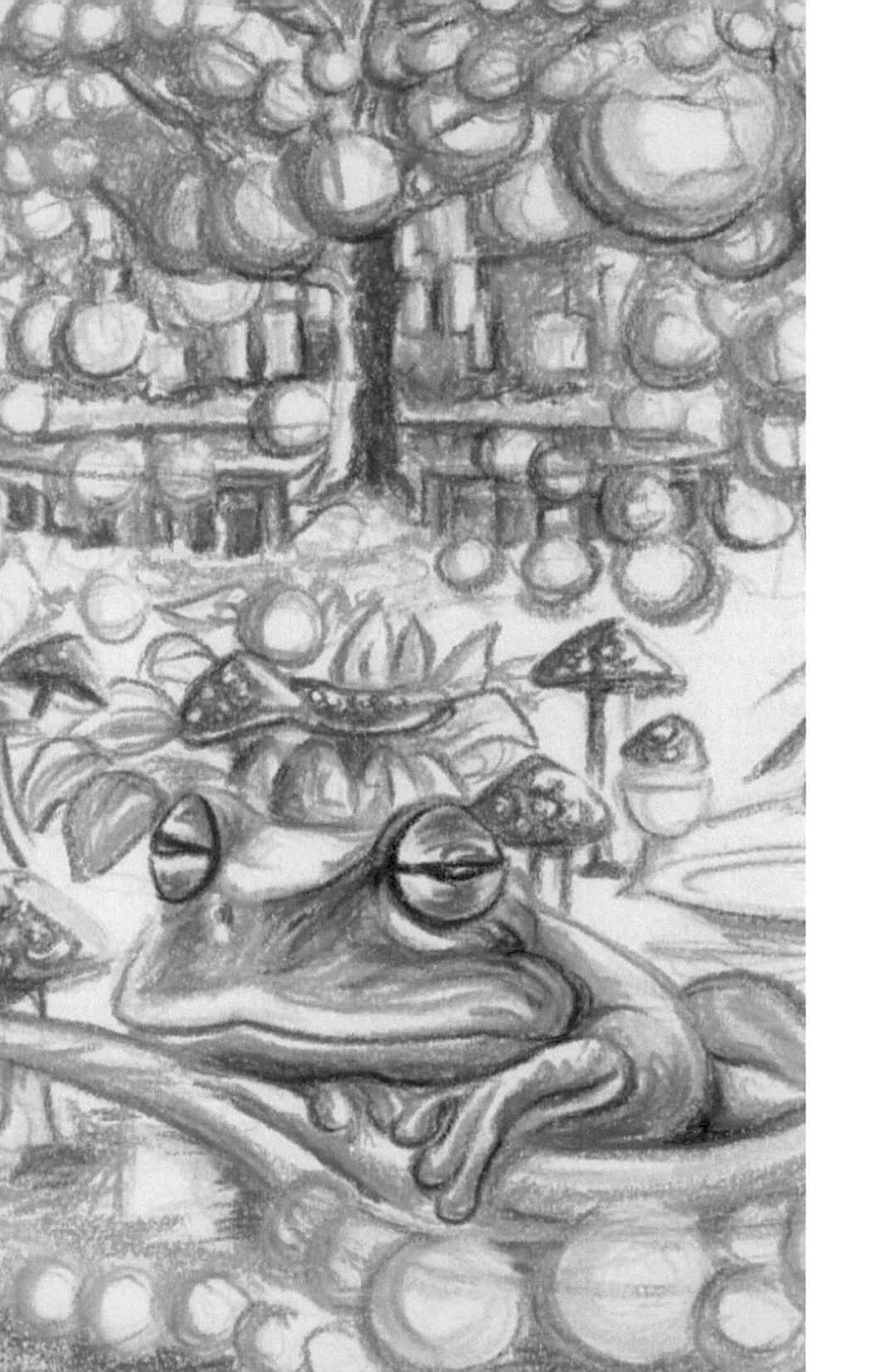

She went and opened the door, and the frog hopped in,

following her all the way to her chair.

There he sat and called: "Lift me up to you."

She hesitated until the king finally ordered her to do so.

Once the frog was on the chair,

he wanted to sit on the table, and as he sat there he said:

"Now push your little golden plate closer to me,

so that we can eat together."

She did, but you could see that she didn't like it.

The frog enjoyed it, but almost every bite remained in her throat.

At last he said: "I have eaten my fill and am tired.

Now carry me into your little chamber and make up your silken bed,

and we will go to sleep there."

9

тΛε т∪ʀɴ ᴏʆ Λ∪ᴍΛɴΙт✝

The turning point of humanity - Responsibility

If humanity summons up the courage and communicates the theme of true freedom again (door), a path will be found that will lead every single person back to the rich table of the ancestors.

But it also needs the support and recognition of the real people in the current management positions (...until the king commands). Many entrepreneurs have realized that their companies, their "heritage", actually belongs to the employees and are already accompanying them into self-responsibility.

But, like the king's daughter, many people are still not comfortable with bearing so much responsibility or become too greedy (...little bite in the throat). **People are making demands again, wanting too much of the cake. Feeling like they are in paradise and being carried, only to fall asleep again** (little bed).

This has also happened for many centuries. People go into their vocation with anticipation and motivation and realize that only the way to the top will bring enough knowledge, money and opportunities for change. But once they reach the top, they quickly forget why they have actually taken on so much or why they set off in the first place.

("Lift me up to you.")

How did all the advanced civilizations in the world develop?

Your ancestors traveled the whole world 4000 years ago, they were traders and bringers of knowledge, they knew agriculture, architecture, natural medicine and psychology, cosmology and the electromagnetic connections of life and thus had a very strong connection to the 5 elements. The vanished buildings, stone circles, megalithic cultures, star fortresses and magnificent Tartar buildings are just a few examples from all over the world that bear witness to this in many ages and epochs.

So we also find another truth about the foundation of "Hellenism" in Greece. Helena, also called Minerva, was an honorary mother of Frya's children, your ancestor. This traditional text explains the differences between the two cultural systems.

Helenja (Minerva) speaks:

"I don't know any gods who are evil. That's why I can't ask if they want to become better.

I know one god, that is Wralda's spirit (guest), but because he is good (god), he does nothing evil.

Then where does the evil come from? - Asked the priests

All evil comes from you and from the stupidity of people who allow themselves to be caught by you.

Then why does he not ward off evil?

Frya has set us on the path and the Kroder (time) must do the rest. There is advice and help to be found in all misfortune. But Wralda wants us to search for ourselves. That we may become strong and wise. If we do not want that, then he (Vralda) will let our hesitation roll out, so that we may know what follows wise deeds and what follows foolish deeds.

Then a prince said:

I should think it would be better to resist it.

Perhaps, replied Helenja. Because then the people will remain like tamed sheep. You and the priests will want to herd them. But also shear them and lead them to the slaughter. But that's not what Vralda's spirit wants.

He wants us to help each other. But he also wants everyone to be free and wise. That is also our will. That is why our people, their princes, counts, counselors and all lords, bosses and masters choose from the wisest of the good people. That everyone may do his best to become wise and good. We should know and teach the nations to act in this way. That being wise and acting wisely alone leads to bliss.

Princes: "How are we to persuade all the people who are under our rule to do this?"

Helenja said: "The sparrows follow the sower, the peoples their good princes. Therefore you have to start by making yourselves so pure that you can turn your eyes inwards and outwards without becoming ashamed of your own conscience. But instead of making the people pure, you have invented filthy, rotten feasts at which the people drink for so long that they end up digging in the mud like wild boars, so that you have to pay for your filthy, rotten desires."

Text excerpt: Oera-Linda

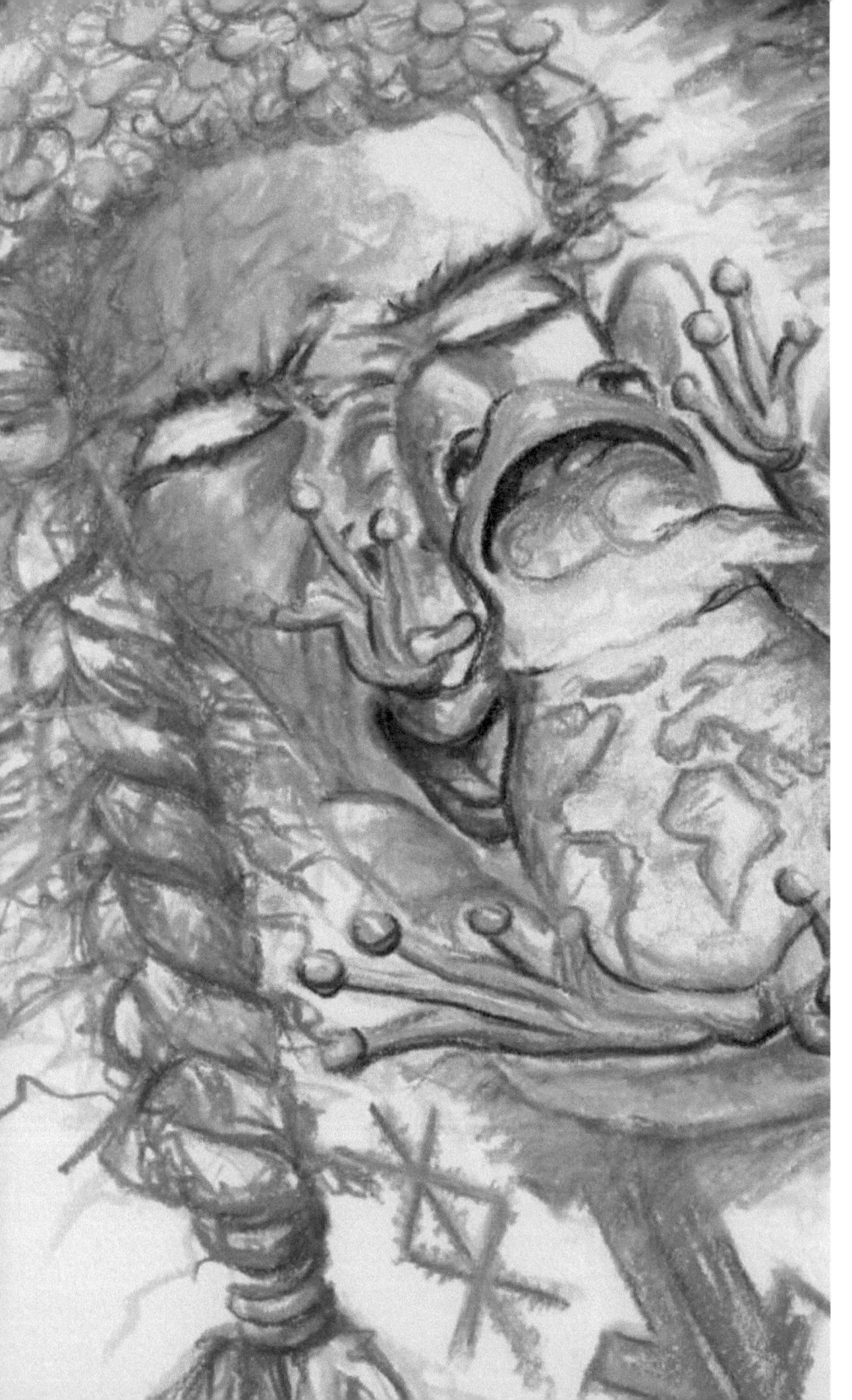

The king's daughter began to weep and was afraid

of the cold frog, which she dared not touch and

who was now to sleep in her beautiful, pure bed.

But the king was angry and said:

"Whoever helped you when you were in need,

you shall not despise him afterward."

Then she grabbed him with two fingers, carried him up and

sat him down in a corner.

But as she lay in bed, he crawled up and said:

"I am tired, I want to sleep as well as you,

Lift me up or I'll tell your father."

Then she became bitterly angry, picked him up and

and threw him against the wall with all her might:

"Now you'll have peace, you nasty frog."

10

THE TURNING OF THE WORLDS

The turning of the worlds - The Ragnarök

Humanity is crying again. Good people with ideals and goals betray themselves and others when they have achieved their own goals. They become cold and unfeeling and - now themselves at the top - allow themselves to be carried like kings.

The king, cosmos - has experienced and watched this game thousands of times. His "wrath" has been expressed and warned through cataclysms, pole jumps and catastrophes.

The two fingers [59] and the corner [60], are today's indication of the fatal efforts of recent generations to improve their own lives through external intelligence. The development of the computer age was driven forward in order to relieve people of "work" through digital systems. That was the thinking.

Technology as a new "slave culture for humans", which was supposed to make life easier for everyone, also became a new prison. New passions and addictions (tired, sleeping) have developed, laziness, dependency, destruction and surveillance have increased. A single solar impulse, however, paralyzes humanity and all systems. It has learned nothing from the past and fear is turning into more and more anger. The earth will - once again - hit the wall, as historical records show. Your ancestors call it Ragnarök - the fate of the mighty.

So will the next, now ongoing (nasty) Ragnarök [61] This process has been initiated and is happening on several levels: personal, social, human, planetary and cosmic. Because it doesn't just affect each individual, but the whole of humanity and the planet.

---

[59] Two (duality, dual = 0+1, off, on), finger (digital = lat. finger) = binary "computer system"

[60] Corner (technology)

[61] Ragnarök: Ragnarök - The Turning of the World - Fate of the Gods - Twilight of the Gods, Fate of the Mighty, The Battle of the Gods against the Giants, Ragna, Rig, Radiant "God = Good", - rök "Cause, Sense of Origin". Your world will change completely. It is a turn to the good path to the cause and the meaning of your origin. The Ragnarök is the end of deception, illusion and duality.
Natural duality = Asen against Vanen = human spirit against nature spirit
Planetary duality = Freyr versus Surt = planetary spirit of the earth; bravery versus (fire) destroyer of worlds
Spiritual duality = Odin vs. wolf = spirit vs. spiritual fears
Emotional duality = Thor vs. Midgard Serpent = Emotions (electrical thoughts, lightning) vs. physical fears, giant mirage
Moral duality = Loki vs. Heimdahl = deception vs. respect and ostracism
Life duality = Garm vs. Tyr = The hound that guards the gate of Hel, Queen of Death, vs. "A divine power"

The wall [62] is the Ragnarök - the beginning of neutrality.

The frog, still held in his hypnotic sleep, experiences a painful awakening. This is described very well and in detail in the Ragnarök of Norse mythology.

The times have proven that mankind first had to drive the world against the wall in order to realize that the earth is a living being. We are living in such a time again. It is happening now.

The RAGNARÖK is what explains the way out of the dilemma of this world.

The construct we were born into. The illusion of duality.
The contradiction between gods and the forces of nature and the alienation of one's own being from oneself.

The Ragnarök also refers to cosmic connections and cycles in two different worlds, the spiritual and the material. The war of the Aesir and the Vanen refers to the two systems that exist on this earth, the class and the circle culture.

But crucially and essentially it is about the inner struggle within ourselves. It is the decisive wisdom for a more peaceful inner life, with ourselves and with all others. It is the crossroads that we inevitably have to walk. But only what we experience ourselves, our own path, can bring about change.

---

[62] Wall = W - Vaner, A - Asen, N - Knowledge, D - Drink
Ragnarök: The end of deception is also the beginning of the ancient knowledge of the greatest power for man and mankind.

Neutrality
This is the secret of nature: neutrality. We come from the neutral and everything around us is neutral. Neutrality is the only way of spirit and matter. In the physical and mental training of future generations, this path will be the only sensible one.

"The end of Ragnarök is also the beginning of a new world. The earth rises again, green and fertile. The Asen Baldr (light - balps, bold, brave balts = white) and Hödr (shadow) return from Hel (unconsciousness), Widar (fighter of nature) and Wali (courage and wisdom) have survived, also Thor's sons Magnis (magnetism) and Modi (courage). These surviving gods are all gods of the second generation, i.e. sons of Odin and Thor. Two humans have also survived, Lif (giving energy = positive +) and Leifþrasir (Lifa = life + pra = longing = receiving energy = negative -), from whom a whole new human race is descended. Finally, the daughter (matriarchy) of the sun (earth) takes over the ways of her mother." The existing Aesir after Ragnarök live in Idawöllr "Idafeld" (Ida = source, origin, Greek idea = archetype, according to Plato "idein" = to see, to recognize).

The common meaning of the myths is also explained here by their simplicity. "If you want to hide something, it's best to place it in plain sight, right in front of your nose. No one will suspect it there."

R -	ᚱ	**Journey, Destination**
A -	ᚠ	**Wisdom, Aesir, Ancestors**
G -	ᚷ	**Gift, Present**
N -	ᚻ	**Longing, Energy**
A -	ᚠ	**Wisdom, Aesir, Ancestors**
R -	ᚱ	**Travel, wagon**
O -	ᛜ	**Home, Heritage, Empire, Universe**
K -	ᚲ	**Revelation, Knowledge, Servitude**

„**Your** ᚱ **journey inwards to your** ᚠ **ancestors,**
leads you to the ᚷ **gift of your being,**
your ᚻ **longing.**
The ᚠ **wisdom of the** ᚱ **way**
brings you ᛜ **home**
to the ᚲ **knowledge of your inheritance."**
Guido Eickhoff

If you let the illusion of duality initiated by the magicians die, your path will be a much more conscious and free one. If conscience is to move back into the world, it can only start with you. There is no duality of life and death, everything is a cycle. Death is merely a good business model. There is no need for dogma or morality if the being in everyone is conscientious.

The Ragnarök (turning of the world) of the earth
In our true history, we repeatedly find catastrophes, floods and conflagrations that the world has experienced in its cosmic cycles. Similar to the cataclysms and cycles of the earth, which have already occurred several times through pole jumps, which are now scientifically proven. In Europe, the old land went under, the old country, which is also Atlantis. In the present time, we expect six cosmic cycles to occur simultaneously.

The Ragnarök of humanity
The war of the Aesir against the Vans. Civilized peoples in an invasion war of destruction and lies. Another Ragnarök was the migration of peoples, the Huns, Magyars (Hungarians) and many other invasions of the world. Finally, the Romans, who repeatedly invaded the peaceful land. Subjugation and slavery became more and more widespread. Nature was destroyed by them and deception and lies were spread. Conscience was almost completely extinguished and the wisdom of the European indigenous peoples disappeared. Until the Ragnarök of the individual began. Observe the world and you will recognize the repetitions, in a different way.

The Ragnarök of man
Every person also experiences their own personal Ragnarök.
Through the loss and suppression of the old indigenous teachings, people lost their footing. We see the symptoms all over the planet and also in the "civilized" world. Often a hypnotized person is only awakened when dramatic things happen. This has happened to many people in their lives. They have realized that they have followed lies and acted against their own nature. It is like a hard impact in which they realize from one moment to the next that the freedom they lived in was not real freedom. What these people then experience is their own Ragnarök. This impact is described in the Völuspá. It is part of the human instinct not to want to see this, because the fear of the new and unknown is often much greater. This is why our ancestors left their clues in myths and legends.

The realization of man, the end of his own deception, the path to conscience and thus the end of deception in the world. It is hidden in your genes. You just have to listen to the voice.

Neutrality
This is the secret of nature. Neutrality. We come from the neutral and everything around us is neutral. Neutrality is the only way of spirit and matter. In the physical and mental training of future generations, this path will be the only sensible one.

But when he *fell down*, he was not a frog,

but a king's son with

beautiful and kind eyes.

He was now, according to her elders will

her dear companion and *husband*.

Then he told her

he had been *cursed* by an evil magician,

and no one could have saved him from the *well* but her alone, and

tomorrow they wanted to go to his kingdom together.

TΛε ЅOᴸUTION

The solution

It is like waking up from a bad dream.

In the present world, man realizes that he has been bewitched by faith and domination as if by a magician (cursed).

Already at birth, we come from higher noble worlds and fall into a deep darkness of matter. Through the creation of idols, gods and idols, false science, false priests and false leaders.

It is the division and separation of humanity that can be redeemed. It is the division and separation of generations that can be redeemed. It is the inner split and division of the individual that can be redeemed. It is the hard realization that what has been separated over generations must be united. The marriage (consort) of the different poles and thus the beginning of the high time of the coming humanity, when everyone starts with themselves.

I have something to tell you.
A truth about you that you might not want to hear.

"You were adopted."

Until a few years ago, Indigenous children in America and Australia were still being forcibly adopted. For over 600 years, the free and natural culture has been systematically destroyed. The same thing happened and is still happening in Europe today, only "in different clothes" and for over 2000 years.

Your whole family was adopted. Generations of children were adopted without ever knowing it. But you didn't know any different. And yet perhaps there was also a feeling inside you? That something is not right in this life. It feels "wrong". If you ask adopted children and adults, they know exactly this feeling. Everything is ok, but something doesn't seem right, it's exactly this feeling.

People are not made for this kind of life.
It makes them sick on all levels.

Take all the stories in all the movies, they've been twisted. You will look at stories and movies differently if you accept it for yourself. But don't worry. Even the word "adopted" has been twisted.

It actually means "chosen".

You are the offspring and descendant of the highest cultural civilizations on earth. The earth and over 350 million indigenous people are just waiting for you and the rest of humanity to wake up.

Man will be disenchanted when humanity once again lives in unity, in the circle, in virtue and responsibility. Then he can once again experience an age of peace, freedom and prosperity in a decentralized social and economic culture.

When we understand the principles of the indigenous natural sciences again, from which the mystery schools, today's philosophies and sciences emerged in the first place, we come to our own origin.

The one original knowledge, the original source, was distributed and hidden in all four cardinal directions. Each cardinal point had a focal point.
Now it is time to reunite this knowledge so that responsible people can combine it and implement it for the benefit of humanity. In the East the knowledge of the energy body = soul, in the West the forces of nature and earth connection = body, in the South the rhythm and the primal force = emotion, only the North (Europe and Russia) = the spirit, has lost much through the split. Here in Europe, the circle must close again. Our task is to reactivate our primal knowledge and connect with the others.

Only when the human being within himself and humanity together come back full circle [63] and come together in harmony, unimagined forces can unfold again.

Harmony and coherence [64], the union of all the indigenous people of this earth, brings the new marriage (consort) of this world. The coherence in the brain, the coherence of brain and heart in the body, the coherence of our own male and female principles, the coherence of the different people, the coherence of man and nature, the coherence of earth and cosmos.

The universes, planets, all people, all living beings are parts of life in this cosmos and in you, the king's child. No being is higher or lower in rank than another. Only justice can guarantee this natural balance and peace. Only this ecological and economic balance can maintain freedom and lead to prosperity for all.

Only then can the phoenix rise up again and the deer ("You are called upon to take the lead.") within you make itself known.

---

[63] The circle is our medicine wheel. A symbol for the energy wheel, the stone circle and the energy is the medicine of our lives. The stone circle, the Yule wheel, the energy wheel, the indigenous teaching of our culture.
[64] Coherence (Latin: cohaerere = to hang together)

Then they fell asleep, and the next morning,

when the sun woke them up, a wagon drove up,

with eight white horses,

They had white ostrich feathers on their heads and

walked in golden chains, and

behind stood the young king's servant,

that was the faithful Henry.

Faithful Henry had been so saddened

when his master had been turned into a frog

that he had three iron bands put around his heart

so that it would not burst with pain and sadness.

But the carriage was to take the young king to his kingdom.

Faithful Henry lifted them both in,

stood in the back again and

was full of joy at his deliverance.

12

TﾍE INSIDERS

The initiates

The cosmic human being.

With the knowledge of the background of the Frog King, you too will become an initiate. This is one of the most important symbols of faithful Henry.

The return of indigenous European social, educational and economic culture and indigenous consciousness.

Faithful Henry is the symbol for the ancient wisdom that is in your genes, as part of the entire cosmos. It has never been lost. It is faithful. Faithful Henry, like a letter carrier on a chariot, like Heimdall with his horn or Hermes with his wings. He is the healing of humanity, he proclaims and brings you back to your home, your origin, your cradle (chariot) from which you sprang. Faithful Henry is also the Heimdall who reconnects the knowledge of the spiritual and material worlds. He is the one who triggers Ragnarök with his Gjallahorn, he is also our conscience. He always remains faithful to us.

The "faithful" is also trust, courage and action. It is repentance. There are so many facets to the word alone.

The 8 horses, Heimdall the eighth, the Möbius strip and Odin's [65] Horse Sleipnir with its 8 legs or the 8 spokes of the wheel is the cosmic spiral. It can be found in all animals, plants and in your genetic helix spiral. The indigenous. It is the symbol of infinity. It is the cosmic consciousness and the consciousness (white horse) itself that will bring the humans back home. It is the "beginning at the beginning" as we find it again in the signs of the children of Frya.

Once humanity approaches the old teachings again, recognizes and experiences them, regains its conscience, its world view, its self-mastery (golden chains), self-empowerment and personal responsibility will be completely different.

She will find her way back and rebuild a positive future with the great knowledge of our ancestors.

---

[65] Odin is your breath, the connection to everything.

If today's science, the cosmic human being and the cosmic principles are included again, it will be a responsible part of a breathtaking future. If it is not misdirected and used unscrupulously.

What has been created so far was only a part of what humanity is capable of. If it resists the next temptation of "higher powers" through digitalization, transhumanization and artificially created intelligence, it can, like Heimdall, regain its "cosmic intelligence" (Reich). In this way, every human being will have a large share in the golden future of the next 7 generations.

The three iron bands around the heart are our own bands (trauma, pain, powerlessness) that we have placed around our hearts. The three iron rings are the three ages. It is also the fragmentation and suppression of the other three remaining ancient indigenous teachings of the "heart" of all indigenous peoples. The "spirit" or better the light, energy science of all suppressed indigenous cultures.

The energy of spirit/conscience/fire in the North, Europe.
The energy of souls/density/dimensions/water in the East, Asia.
The energy of the body/nature/earth in the West, America.
The energy of community/rhythm/air in the South, Africa.

This is the knowledge of the circle culture, the stone circle.

When we have internalized the previous, we will understand why it is only through the union of all Indigenous Peoples that we can move into the next age.
The true bonds must be reconnected.
The iron bands of duality must finally break.

There are still around 500 million people in the world who identify themselves as indigenous and continue to draw attention to themselves on many continents. Only in Europe, where the knowledge that was brought to them comes from, has everything been completely wiped out. If Europe does not find its way back to its old roots, then the whole world is finished.

The story is told so often now and yet mankind only listens to the false magicians and princes. They have been told that there must be a savior. This too is a psychological trap of stories. Because the original meaning of stories has not been conveyed. Because you are the Frog Prince, you are faithful Henry and the King's daughter, the King. You are the fountain and the golden ball, the lime tree and the genealogical table. You are the only hero's journey to which you must set out and seek your equal. Take the rainbow bridge to the people of conscience.

Heinrich is the key to understanding the scientific connections between spirit and matter = nature. Spirit, however, is not to be understood as philosophy, but as scientific knowledge of the invisible electromagnetic connections of light on all levels (cosmic, planetary, earthly, natural, human, cellular, energetic, ...).

The middle class is the bridge that must re-form in this age. The middle class is the force of neutrality. Only the synergy of the inherent entities of a natural community of culture and life will bring about a fruitful future. The combination of spirit (conscience) and matter (energy).

"All humans are descendants of tribal peoples who were spiritually alive and closely connected to the natural world, children of Mother Earth. As tribal people, we knew who we were, we knew where we were, and we knew our destiny. The sacred perception of reality remains alive and well in our genetic memory. We carry it within us, mostly in a dusty box in the attic of our minds, but it is accessible."
John Trudell

Image: "European mittelstand (middle-stand: people who stand for the middle) must make a decision. - Guido Eickhoff"

And when they had gone some way,

the king's son heard a crash behind him,

as if something had broken. Then he turned around and called out:

"Heinrich, the wagon is breaking!"

"No, Lord, not the wagon,

It's a ribbon from my heart,

That lay there in great pain,

When you sat in the well,

When you were a frog."

Once more and once more there was a crash on the way,

and the king's son always thought the carriage was breaking up, and

but it was only the ribbons

that broke from the heart of faithful Henry,

because his lord was redeemed and happy.

13

TΛƐ RƐBIRTΛ

The rebirth

It is now up to us adults, the people in the middle, the craftsmen and traders, the workers and service providers and their children, who have received a good education, to come together again to form a family, a tribe. The generations that belong together again and achieve a common goal.

It is up to those who courageously lead the way and explore and implement new paths. Those who build a new educational, economic and social culture that reaches back to the old times. Who build unifying communities that offer a safe home to all people on this living and feeling being, our earth.

The journey into the new future can scare **people** (the wagon breaks). If man can cast off the bands (band of my heart) that he has put on himself - through false belief, false power and false education. Then he will never again have the feeling of being alone and he will feel the connection that has always existed. The more people come together, the stronger the community.

We create small kingdoms again, starting in families, companies, villages and regions, where peace, freedom and justice are once again at the center (middle class). Then, with the restored conscience of our ancestors and future generations, we can create places for our children and grandchildren where their full potential and gifts have the opportunity to mature.

An environment in which they can thrive. We need small kingdoms that combine the old and the new. It is the beginning of a new age that will transform the future into a golden one. Let's start the journey together.

We take up our inheritance of the joyful (Lord) people now.

As children of Frya, the free people.

It is in your genes.

You are INDIGENOUS.

The conclusion is the key.

So this fairy tale is a reminder and a cornucopia of peaceful solutions from your ancestors.

To find and walk the path out of your own darkness. To regain your own connectedness, strength, courage, pride and freedom in order to unite the worldwide connection of all human peoples, the indigenous, the nature-born and to make peace.

To continue the outstanding developments of today's society and to accompany it into a free, liberal and just cultural evolution. To bring the hidden legacy of your ancestral parents back into the circle and selflessly prepare the golden age for the next seven generations with more conscience.

It is not enough to think it. We have to do it.

All the indigenous people of the world are just waiting for the Europeans to wake up from their "magic sleep" and recognize the right, the human right, and identify themselves as indigenous people in order to stand up together for peace in this world and revive the "**consciousness of the circle**".

THANK YOU!

Guido Eickhoff

Sources, book list

(Extract)

The Oera Linda Book, William R. Sandbach 1876
The Oera Linda Book: From a Manuscript of the Thirteenth Century, William R. Sandbach, Cornelis Over De Linden, J. G. Ottema, 1876
The Ura Linda Chronicle, Hermann Wirth, 1933
Chronology of the Ura Linda Chronicle, Gerd Simon, 2005
The Oera Linda manuscripts: The early history of Europe, Harm Menkens, 2022
Codex Oera Linda, Jan Ott, 2023
The Oera Linda Project, Oera Linda, Youtube channel, 2010
Video series about the Oera Linda manuscripts, Die Zuversicht, YouTube channel, 2020
The enigma of the Danube civilization. The discovery of Europe's oldest advanced civilization, Harald Haarmann, 2011

Children's and Household Tales, Brothers Grimm, 1812
The secret language of German fairy tales, Werner von Bülow, 1925
The Masks of Odin, Elsa Brita Titchenell 1985
German legends, Brothers Grimm, 1816
Weltbilderschütterung - The correct decipherment of hieroglyphic writing, Erhard Landmann, 1993
Vatan - the path of the north, Edmund von Hollander, 2021
Parzival, Wolfram Eschenbach, around 1200
Siegfried saga, Nibelungenlied, (1220-1250)
Barbarossa saga, German legends, Brothers Grimm, 1816
The Edda, Karl Simrock 1851
Kalewala, the Finnish national epic, Elias Lönnrot, translated by Anton Schiefner, 1835
The Bock Saga: An introduction, Carl Borgen, 2019
The Bock Saga, an introduction, audiobooks for reflection, Youtube channel, 2019
Ragnarök: Twilight of the gods and the end of the world in Norse literature, Stefanie Würth, 2002
The North Pole as a homeland for peoples, Dr. Georg Biedenkapp, 1906
High time of mankind, Rudolf John Gorsleben, 1930
The Secret of the Hyperboreans, Victor K. Wendt, 1984
Atlantis, Edda and Bible, Hermann Wieland, 2001
King Arthur in Hyperborea and the Arctic Mudflow Catastrophe, The Confidence Youtube Channel, 2020
Santia Weden Perunas, Ancestral heritage Germania, Alexander Hinewitsch
The Weden Book of Light, Ancestral Heritage Germania, Alexander Hinewitsch
Tribal source, Oleg, Elena Pankov, 2012
Slavic Aryan Vedas, Eugen von Belo-Vod'e, Youtube channel, 2013
Tartaria: Hidden History Revealed, Larry Fitzgerald, 2023
The One World Tartarians (black and white): 1st, James Lee, 2022
The Third Eye and the Origin of Humanity, Ernst Muldaschev, 2001
The Great Mahabharata, 1st book, Adi Parva, "The Book of Origins", Kisari Mohan Ganguli (1883-1896) and Manmatha Nath Dutt (1895-1905), translation Undine & Jens 2009
Germania, Tacitus, Johann Christoph Schlüter, 1821

Awareness of the circle, Thomas Arculeo, Guido Eickhoff, 2024
Peaceful Solutions, Volumes 1-5, Thomas Arculeo 2023/2024
To Become a Human Being: The Message of Tadodaho Chief Leon Shenandoah, by Steve Wall, Leon Shenandoah, 2002
"Deganawidah, the Peacemaker" - White Roots of Peace: Iroquois Book of Life: The Iroquois Book of Life, Paul A. W. Wallace , 1994
Iroquois and Democracy, A Contribution to the Sociology of Intercultural Communication, Thomas Wagner, 2004
The myth of democracy - Ancient models of rule between the principle of equality and the elite principle, Harald Haarmann, 2013
The pharmacy of Manitou, Heinz-Josef Stammel, 1986
The medicine wheel, Peter Kirschner, 2019
Babaji - Kriya Yoga and the 18 Siddhas, Marshall Govindan, 2010
Tao Te King, Lao Tzu, 6th century BC
Quetzalcoatl - the Feathered Serpent - The Birth of a Legend, Angelika Neumann, 2022
Quetzalcoatl: The History and Legacy of the Feathered Serpent God in Mesoamerican Mythology, Charles River Editors, 2019
The Odyssey of Aristotle, Wendelin von Winckelstein, 2005

Analyses and Assessment of Gateway Process, Department Of Defence USA, www.cia.gov, 1983, released 2003
Secret of the Light, Walter Russell (1875 - 1963), 2022
Ultimate Collection, William Walker Atkinson (1862 - 1932), 2016
My inventions, Nicola Tesla 1856, 2019
The Repulsine, Impusion_Heft 036_10969, Viktor Schauberger,1969
The Universe in the Light of Modern Physics, Max Planck;1931
The Decoding of the Universe: The Key Came at the Right Time, Nassim Haramein, 2011
The Language of our DNA - Scalar Energy, Jere Rivera-Dugenio, Ph.D., 2019
The Evolution of Consciousness into Matter, Jere Rivera-Dugenio, Ph.D. 2019
The Zero Point Field, Lynne McTaggart, 2002
The decoding of the Vedas, Christian Knopke, 2013
The Apocalypse of God, A Revelation, Alexander Laurent, 2012
Psychology of the masses, Gustave Le Bon, 2009
Clinical hypnosis and hypnotherapy: practical textbook for training, Agnes Kaiser Rekkas, 2013
The message of water, Masaru Emoto, 2010
Trees & the healing power of the forest, Adelheid Lingg, 2016

Universal Declaration of Human Rights,
www.unric.org/de/allgemeine-erklaerung-menschenrechte/
Declaration on the Rights of Indigenous Peoples, UNDRIP, www.un.org
Documentation, Research and Information Center for Indigenous Peoples, www.docip.org
European Indigenous Development Center, EIDC.mittelstand.de
LIVING CIRCLE, "Living Circle" model campus, LIVING-CIRCLE.mittelstand.de

Our initiatives

MARKTPLATZ.mittelstand.de
Platform for the SME sector.
A community that seeks to join forces.

LIVING-CIRCLE.mittelstand.de
The Living Circle was initiated to build a nourishing and value-creating culture of living based on the forgotten wisdom of our traditional European science and culture. With the aim of strengthening the middle class for the challenging future. To initiate new essentials of relationship, education, health and communication and to contribute naturally to the revitalization of our society and to reconnect people, nature, work and life.

EIDC.mittelstand.de
The EIDC provides the new seed with the "LIVING CIRCLE" as a blueprint of traditional European natural sciences in connection with the New Sciences, as a sustainable growth principle at all levels of a modern cultural development, for a thriving development of the individual up to intelligent cities and communities.

The "LIVING CIRCLE" is the basic "concept" that can be replicated and used in schools and governing bodies, in communities and in personal development.

The EIDC is supported by qualified bodies such as 4 Worlds International, UN, Unesco, European Union (Docip) to set the course in the field of Global Urban Development.

BILDUNG.mittelstand.de
Training and seminar program:
LIVING CIRCLE - Awareness of the circle - Future program "Indigenous Europe".
ACADEMY FOR INDIGENOUS EUROPE

BERATUNG.mittelstand.de
Information, inquiries:
info@mittelstand.de

A project by LIVING-CIRCLE.mittelstand.de

„The Frog King and the children of Frya"

Book orders: "The Frog King and the Children of Frya"
www.mittelstand.de/derfroschkoenig

Book orders
www.mittelstand.de/shop
www.mittelstand.de/buecher
buecher@mittelstand.de

Contact us
Guido Eickhoff
info@mittelstand.de

Merchandising
www.mittelstand.de/shop
European Native

Become a supporter:
EIDC.mittelstand.de

Books - LIVING-CIRCLE.mittelstand.de:

www.mittelstand.de/shop

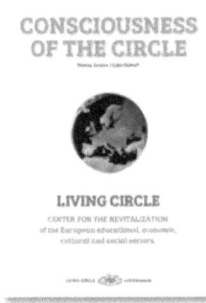

ISBN: 9783759750914

LIVING CIRCLE - Consciousness of the circle
MODEL CAMPUS FOR THE REVITALIZATION
of the European economic, cultural and social system.

The model campus for a thriving SME sector.
The education-oriented center for a creative resource community.
Shaping the future - With the requirements of tomorrow
Exploit the opportunities of today and integrate them in a timely manner.
Taking responsibility today for the life values of generations to come.

ISBN: 9783759759122

Peaceful solutions
The self-experiential introduction to the legacy of the Druids and Elders of the world. The entire series of books is a teaching path of the ancient way of the masters, as it was passed on orally in the past.
The author translates in writing what his masters have explained to him through oral traditions and examples of action.

Volume - 1 - Intro
Volume - 2 - I
Volume - 3 - We
Volume - 4 - The 5 Elements
Volume - 5 - (0)

...

ISBN: 9783759759603

The Frog King & the children of Frya
- Volume 1

Fairy tales are messages from your ancestors.
The foundations of all peaceful civilizations on this earth.
The history of Europe and its circular culture.
The legacy of Europe's indigenous culture,
explained in detail using language, codes and images.

The Frog King & the teachings of the children of Frya
- Volume 2

The knowledge of indigenous European natural science and the
the background of their circular culture was the basis
of all peaceful civilizations. It is time to bring this knowledge
and the teachings deeper into people's consciousness again.
The Frog Prince is the symbol for this process.
Fairy tales are messages from your ancestors.
The legacy of Europe's indigenous culture.

ISBN:9783759760012

A dandellon seed goes on a journey
Children's book

A hero's journey through the elements of life.
It shows courage, self-knowledge,
the inner power and the rich paths that life offers.
The story gives us strength and makes us realize
how we can grow from apparent vulnerability
to an unusual greatness.
It is the impulse to take a closer look at the world
and to take a closer look.
It is the dragon within us that is awakened and
the scientific wisdom of our ancestors,
to which wonderful being we are connected.

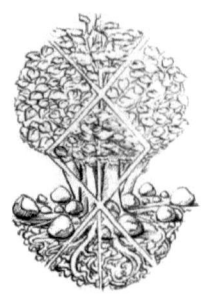

EUROPEAN ✳ NATIVE